INDUSTRY ACT 1975

by

THOMAS SHARPE

of Lincoln's Inn, Barrister, Lecturer in Law, University of Sussex

LONDON
BUTTERWORTHS
1976

Annotated Legislation Service Volume 241

ENGLAND
Butterworth & Co. (Publishers) Ltd.
London: 88 Kingsway, London WC2B 6AB

AUSTRALIA
Butterworths Pty. Ltd.
Sydney: 586 Pacific Highway, Chatswood, NSW 2067
Also at Melbourne, Brisbane, Adelaide and Perth

CANADA
Butterworth & Co. (Canada) Ltd.
Toronto: 2265 Midland Avenue, Scarborough, M1P 4S1

NEW ZEALAND
Butterworths of New Zealand Ltd.
Wellington: 26–28 Waring Taylor Street, Wellington 1

SOUTH AFRICA
Butterworth & Co. (South Africa) (Pty.) Ltd.
Durban: 152–154 Gale Street, Durban

U.S.A.
Butterworth & Co. (Publishers) Inc.
Boston: 19 Cummings Park, Woburn, Mass. 01801

ISBN 0 406 54753 X

PREFACE

This book is offered as an aid to those whose business it is to understand the Industry Act 1975, though I hope it will be of interest also to students of economics and industrial policy.

I have attempted to place the Act in context by describing previous legislation dealing with selective government intervention in the economy, and, in particular, certain sections of the Industry Act 1972. In view of the relatively undeveloped state of economic law in the United Kingdom I took the opportunity to consider the ways in which the exercise of the public powers described here may affect the law generally.

The Act is a most interesting piece of legislation. Its parliamentary passage acted as a "seismograph, registering the force of political tremors elsewhere". The machinations surrounding the final inevitable compromise afforded the connoisseur some pleasure, though causing the textwriter some headache. No Bill has proved so destructive of ministers; few Bills can have had such an able Committee scrutinizing them (a Committee, incidentally, which did not feel the necessity to divide on party lines all the time).

Yet many lawyers will be, or ought to be, disappointed. Drawing on recently established precedents the Act is replete with subjective powers, which, unless the courts prove unusually and perhaps unwisely "active", will insulate ministerial decisions from judicial review. Accompanying the virtual absence of judicial review, the party political structure and pressures on parliamentary time render parliamentary approval, in other than a purely formal sense, a polite fiction. One can understand ministerial reluctance to upset a balance which manifestly favours the Government and civil servants who, readily and properly, point to the lack of interest among lawyers in the creation and sensitive use of a legal framework in the conduct of economic policy.

This is a melancholy conclusion. It was foreseen by Professor Daintith in his vision of ". . . the golden metwand of the law reduced to an economist's bludgeon, and lawyers themselves reduced to mere technicians of whom a select few, the Parliamentary draftsmen, are themselves planning the obsolescence of the rest".

September 1976

THOMAS SHARPE

NOTES

1. Frequent reference is made in the text to the Standard Industrial Classification. For further information consult *Standard Industrial Classification—Alphabetical List of Industries* (revised 1968) 2nd impression 1974, H.M.S.O.

2. An Appendix contains the list of N.E.B. holdings on 31 August 1976.

3. As a result of increasing commitments to provide selective financial assistance to industry and of the effects of inflation on the limits imposed under s. 8 (7) of the Industry Act 1972, the Government introduced on 9 April 1976 an amendment Bill to raise the initial limit for the provision of financial assistance under s. 8 of that Act from £150m to £600m and the overall limit from £550m to £1600m. See the Secretary of State's speech on the Second Reading, HC Deb (1975–6) 910 c. 579.

4. The Industry Act 1975 came into force on 20th November 1975 (Industry Act (Commencement) Order 1975 S.I. No. 1881).

CONTENTS

TABLE OF STATUTES

References in this Table to "Statutes" are to Halsbury's Statutes of England (Third Edition) showing the volume and page at which the annotated text of the Act will be found.

Paragraph references printed in bold type indicate where the Industry Act 1975 is set out.

vii

Table of Statutes

CHAPTER 1

INTRODUCTION

The proposition that the free play of market forces would result in an arcadia of economic harmony is not one that has ever commanded universal acceptance. Indeed, the fact of political responsibility for industrial success and the efficient provision of goods and services has long been recognised. This political responsibility has sometimes taken the form of outright nationalisation of an industry or a significant proportion of it, or less dramatically, by the provision of State subsidies, in the form of allowances or grants, to encourage a higher level of investment and the provision of more jobs. The establishment of the National Enterprise Board, the statutory corporation created by the Industry Act 1975, marks the latest of several experiments designed to bring Government influence to bear more closely on companies, without necessarily taking the enterprises into public ownership or risking the lack of control implicit in investment and regional incentives. [1]

Previous legislation, notably the Industrial Reorganisation Corporation Act 1966 (A.L.S. Vol. 158), the Industrial Expansion Act 1968 (A.L.S. Vol. 172) and the Industry Act 1972 (A.L.S. Vol. 204), has proved incapable of surviving a change in the political complexion of the Government without repeal or substantial amendment. Nevertheless, the philosophy of the present Act is based upon some very familiar premises: that Britain's industrial performance is "unsatisfactory", that the market mechanism is an inefficient or insufficient means through which industrial "success" can be achieved and that State intervention is *therefore* necessary, in selected instances, to seek an improvement. [2]

INDUSTRIAL REORGANISATION CORPORATION

The I.R.C. created by the Industrial Reorganisation Corporation Act 1966, was designed to encourage the restructuring of industry, normally, though not exclusively, by the encouragement of mergers. The aim was to produce larger, "optimally-sized" industrial units, which the market would not have produced or would have taken an unconscionable time in so producing, if left to its own volition. The functions of the I.R.C. were stated in s. 2: they were to promote, "industrial efficiency and profitability", to assist, "the economy of the United Kingdom", and to "promote or assist the reorganisation or development of any industry". Although the Secretary of State could request the Corporation to, ". . . establish or develop, or promote or assist the establishment or development of any industrial enterprise" (s. 2 (1) (b)) it was left to the Board of the I.R.C. in other matters, ". . . to consider which industries it would be expedient" to concentrate on (s. 2 (2)). Apart from the encouragement of mergers the I.R.C. developed as a catalyst for change, supplying short-term finance, coordinating institutional shareholders in seeking changes within companies and acting as a source of advice to Government departments. Occasionally, it sponsored or actively encouraged takeover bids and committed part of the £150m. which had initially been placed at its disposal in support of one or other of the parties concerned, by purchasing shares in the open market. This was the Corporation's response to a subsidiary of the Swedish company S.K.F., Skefco, bidding for certain elements of the British ball-bearing industry. Similarly, it supported George Kent in its successful takeover of Cambridge Instruments, in preference to competing bids from Rank. Naturally, in so doing the Corporation exercised its discretion and interpreted the public interest in a particular way. [3]

By deciding to support one company at the expense of other companies the I.R.C. adopted what its first Managing Director described disapprovingly as a "tribunal function", without, of course any means of legal redress available to anyone who felt aggrieved by its conduct. [4]

The I.R.C. possessed the attributes of a merchant bank, with the very considerable assets of Government support and £150m. As stated above, it had the power to buy equity in companies. This was not done with the intention of building up a State-owned portfolio of shares in the private sector, but more with the intention of directing funds into particular companies without burdening them with fixed interest debt. Although the Board was seeking more than the original tranche of £150m. at the time of its dissolution (Industry Act 1971, s. 2) the I.R.C.'s purpose was not to become a State holding company, but that it should steadily liquidate assets acquired to finance further developments. In fact, overall, the I.R.C. did not fall far short of earning a commercial return on capital. [5]

INDUSTRIAL EXPANSION ACT 1968

The Industrial Expansion Act 1968 was designed to provide aid in situations where the structure of industry was an obstacle to viability. In addition, the powers granted to the Government obviated the necessity for separate pieces of legislation in order to sanction public expenditure on particular projects. Such projects were styled "industrial investment schemes" and in the eyes of the sponsoring Government were justified because ". . . of a divergence between national and private costs and benefits". The schemes were created by Statutory Instrument, requiring an affirmative resolution, which though permitting Parliamentary discussion did not allow of modification or amendment. Two important examples of schemes facilitated by the Act were the consolidation of the British computer industry (Computers Mergers Scheme 1968, S.I. 1968 No. 990) and the establishment of large scale aluminium smelting capacity in the United Kingdom (Aluminium Industry (Invergordon Project) Scheme 1968, S.I. 1968 No. 1875, Aluminium Industry (Anglesey Project) Scheme 1968, S.I. 1968 No. 1874). In the smelter case, the companies in question received not only the general investment and regional grants available at the time but a fixed interest loan which permitted the companies to purchase a notional portion of power stations constructed by the Scottish Hydro Electric Board and the

Central Electricity Generating Board respectively. Essentially, this purchase of part of electricity generating capacity did not fall into the conventional definition of an asset which could be secured against a loan. Short of a general charge on the parent companies' assets, the Government was the only source of capital. [6]

To ensure expertise in the selection of projects and also to avoid unfair discrimination against companies not involved in an industrial investment scheme, an Advisory Committee was formed consisting of members of the I.R.C., the N.R.D.C. and representatives from industry (s. 5). But the final decision to employ public funds lay with the appropriate minister. There was no delegation of responsibility to a specialist agency such as the I.R.C. or N.E.B. [7]

The Government could acquire an equity shareholding but only in pursuance of an industrial investment scheme, and if the risk of a low commercial return inhibited funds from being offered by the capital market. As the purpose of the Act was to encourage projects where the social benefit was greater than the private benefit (with smelters, the social benefit was the planned saving of foreign exchange as a result of import saving; it is a moot point whether the smelters would have been constructed if the calculations on savings in foreign exchange had been made after the 1967 devaluation), it was likely that most projects would not have been commercially viable and therefore would not have attracted private funds. The Government's ability to acquire equity was further qualified by the requirement that the board of the company would have to consent to the Government purchase. [8]

The shares were held directly by the Government or the appropriate minister and unlike the informal rule adopted by the I.R.C. no time limit was placed on the Government holding (s. 2 (2) (*e*), (3)). It was felt appropriate that the tax-payer should participate in the success of a venture which, by definition, was only possible by virtue of public money and which would be additional to any increased yield from Corporation tax. But for the most part Government assistance was in the form of loans and grants. [9]

INDUSTRY ACT 1972

The Industry Act 1971 repealed the two above mentioned statutes, but it proved impossible to deny political responsibility for industrial affairs, and in 1972 a futher Industry Act was passed, Part II of which sought to provide a general framework for selective government financial assistance to industry. This Act has been extensively amended by the Industry Act 1975, but in its original form a reluctant Government conceded certain limitations to Government involvement, namely, that Government assistance should be the last resort (ss. 7 (4) and 8 (3)), that Government acquisition of loan and share capital should only be with the consent of the company in question (s. 7 (4) and 8 (3) (*a*)) and that such holdings should be disposed of by the Secretary of State ". . . as soon as, in his opinion, it is reasonably practicable to do so . . ." (ss. 7 (5) and 8 (4)). The powers contained in s. 7 apply exclusively to the assisted areas and Northern Ireland, and s. 8 powers refer to the United Kingdom, "or any part or area of the United Kingdom". The purposes for

which assistance may be given are identical for each section but important
consequences follow from the distinction: in the original Act, s. 8 powers were
not to be exercisable after 31st December 1977; no such time limit exists in the
case of s. 7 powers; in s. 8, share acquisitions were limited to 50% of the company's equity share capital (s. 8 (3) (*b*)), under s. 7 there is no such limit; the
original financial limit for general assistance under s. 8 (7) was £150m., no overall
limit was placed on moneys expended under s. 7, and, lastly, for more than £5m.
to be paid in respect of any one project under s. 8, the excess over £5m. has to
be authorised by a resolution of the House of Commons. Parliamentary approval
is not required for expenditure under s. 7.   [**10**]

The Industrial Development Advisory Board is created by s. 9, and it
consists of individuals who have, *inter alia* ". . . shown capacity in, industry
banking, accounting and finance". This Board gives the Secretary of State
guidance on the deployment of the resources at his disposal, but it has an
advisory function only. Once again, as with the Advisory Committee created
under the Industrial Expansion Act 1968, and unlike the I.R.C., the final
decision on aid rests with the Secretary of State. Any departure from the
I.D.A.B.'s recommendation has to be justified by the Secretary of State in a
statement before Parliament, if the Board so requests. In the Annual Report
by the Secretary of State for Industry on the working of the Industry Act
1972 during the year ending 31st March 1975 (HC620 of 1974–5, p. 17), the
Chairman of the I.D.A.B. noticed five instances where though, in the Board's
opinion, the situation did not appear to warrant assistance, the Government
concluded that assistance should be provided. The Board requested the
Secretary of State to make a Parliamentary Statement explaining his decision
on only one occasion.   [**11**]

In summary, the background to the Industry Act 1975 consisted of the
enactments detailed above, and various other lesser pieces of legislation concerned with the problems of specific industries, notably shipbuilding (the
Shipbuilding Industry Act 1967 was repealed by the Industry Act 1972). By
facilitating selective intervention they represented a distinct change of emphasis
from the traditional methods of State control—the manipulation of the commercial environment by monetary and fiscal policies, the provision of incentives
and nationalisation.   [**12**]

Several points can be noted by way of introduction to the Industry Act
1975. Firstly, there has been a steadily increasing tendency for the powers
Government has assumed to become more general, and not to be restricted to
the problems of any one industry. As a concomitant, these powers are not
typically open to judicial review, but are exercisable at the sole discretion of the
ministry or agency concerned. In order to facilitate efficiency, expedition and
consistency, administrative rules have been created which act as a guide to
the way in which the discretion might be exercised. The adherence of the
ministry or agency to such rules would not necessarily render the decision open
to judicial review providing that the rules do not act as a fetter to the exercise
of the appropriate authority's discretion. To be free of judicial interference,
therefore, the minister must practise an open-minded observance of the
department's rules. (See *British Oxygen Co., Ltd.* v. *Minister of Technology*,
[1971] A.C. 610; [1970] 3 All E.R. 165, for an example of an unsuccessful

challenge to the validity of an administrative rule concerning the minimum value of new plant and machinery eligible for an investment grant payable under the Industrial Development Act 1966.) Secondly, there are important differences between the major political parties regarding the means by which Government influence over industry is wielded. In 1966 and again in 1975 the Labour Party delegated the responsibility for selective intervention to a specialist agency, largely independent, endowed with substantial public funds and not directly answerable to Parliament. The Conservatives, by contrast, fearing that such an agency, intervening in the market at its own will, would become a "force of manipulation and coercion" abolished the I.R.C. and chose to create a specialist unit within the Department of Trade and Industry, whose Minister was accountable to Parliament in the normal way. [13]

Notwithstanding this institutional difference, a fundamental difference of approach in the means by which the State exerted its influence was evident. The Conservative Government in its Industry Act 1972 placed numerous qualifications on the right of the State to take equity holdings, important among which was the requirement that such holdings could only be taken with the company's consent. No comparable provision is to be found in the legislation creating the I.R.C. or the N.E.B.

Equally, the Conservatives favoured the granting of loans and guarantees, wherever possible, but Labour Party policy has developed in the direction of seeking equity participation in return for State aid—and indeed, almost to suggest that State aid should *only* be given in return for a State shareholding, thereby contributing to the build up of a State-owned portfolio. [14]

The political debate became rarified during the Industry Act's passage throughout Parliament. The expectations generated in the luxury of opposition created a climate in which much was expected of the Bill, but as we shall see the imaginative and controversial proposals of the White Paper entitled "The Regeneration of British Industry", Cmnd. 5710 (1974), were either compromised or improved, according to political taste. The Government seldom commanded a majority of its own supporters in the Committee, and by the time the bill received the Royal Assent on 12th November 1975, it had performed the novel feat of disposing of the three principal Ministers of the Department of Industry, two of whom were transferred to other ministerial duties, and the third resigned. [15]

CHAPTER 2

THE NATIONAL ENTERPRISE BOARD

ESTABLISHMENT

The National Enterprise Board was established by the s. 1 of the Industry Act 1975. Its membership consists of a Chairman and between eight and sixteen other members, all of whom will be selected by the Secretary of State. Provision is made (s. 1 (4)) for the Secretary of State to appoint a Deputy Chairman or Chairman from among the members of the Board, and the Board, with the approval of the Secretary of State, may appoint a Chief Executive, who may or may not be a member of the Board. [16]

COMPOSITION

No particular capabilities or qualifications are set out in the Act as necessary for membership of the Board, except acceptability to the Secretary of State. The original bill referred to " . . . persons . . . of . . . wide experience . . . capacity in industry, technology, commercial or financial matters, administration or the organisation of workers", but this was dropped in Committee, presumably because it was unnecessarily restrictive. [17]

During the course of the Committee stage, an unusually innovatory Committee sought restrictions on the discretion of the Secretary of State in deciding both the composition of the Board and the tenure of its members. It was suggested that each appointment should be approved by Parliament. This was not carried. The Committee was successful, however, in eventually securing important changes in the traditional practice regarding the disclosure of Board members' private interests. [18]

DISCLOSURE OF INTERESTS

First, Board members are naturally subject to the conventions regarding disclosure of any personal interest they may possess in any matter. But this has long been regarded as a purely "dignified" safeguard, so, in common with recent nationalising statutes, a duty is placed on the Secretary of State (Sch. 1, para. 1) to satisfy himself that any prospective member of the Board shall not have ". . . such financial or other interest as is likely to affect prejudicially the performance of his functions as a member", and to satisfy himself that no such interests are acquired by existing members. A corresponding duty is placed on prospective and existing members to supply any specified information, in order to allow the Secretary of State to make such a statement. [19]

Furthermore, a member who is in any way directly or indirectly interested in a contract made or proposed to be made by the Board, has to disclose the nature of his interest at a meeting of the Board, or failing his attendance, by taking reasonable steps to secure that a notice of his disclosure is taken into consideration and read at such a meeting; the disclosure should be recorded in the minutes of the meeting (Sch. 1, para. 13). A simple declaration that the Board member is also a member of a specified company or firm and should be regarded as interested in any contract made between the N.E.B. and the company is sufficient disclosure of the interest. [**20**]

In respect of other matters which fall to be considered by the Board, the same rules apply except that the Board member in question may at the discretion of the Board participate in the discussion and final decision. This provision would presumably embrace the situation where a company in which a Board member has a stake or some other connection, makes a contract with a company in which the N.E.B. has an interest, but not with the Board itself. This "other matter" must be declared. [**21**]

The provisions described above mark the orthodox requirements of disclosure by members of the boards of statutory corporations. It should be noticed that such disclosure is a private matter, between the individual concerned, the Board, and the Secretary of State. The responsibilities of the N.E.B. extend beyond the normal limit of nationalised industries: for instance, s. 2 (2) (*c*) gives the Board powers to extend public ownership into profitable areas of manufacturing industry. Conflicts of private interest and public responsibility are more likely to arise in those in whom such a power (among many others) is vested, and a reluctant Government was forced to concede the need for the *public* disclosure of Board members' interests (s. 1 (8)). [**22**]

Accordingly, a duty is placed on the Secretary of State to maintain a register of members' financial interests, ". . . as, were they Members of the House of Commons, they would be required to register in accordance with resolutions of that House, any such resolution being construed, in its application to members of the Board, with appropriate modifications". This Register will be found attached to the Board's Annual Report to the Secretary of State, which must be laid before Parliament (Sched. 2, para. 8 (1)–(3)). [**23**]

CROWN PRIVILEGE

The N.E.B. is not entitled to any Crown Privilege. It is not to be regarded as the servant or agent of the Crown, ". . . or as enjoying any status, immunity or privilege of the Crown", and any property held by the Board will not be property of, or property held on behalf of the Crown. This declaration, which is customary in recent statutes establishing similar corporations (Civil Aviation Act 1971, s. 1 (4); Industrial Reorganisation Corporation Act 1966, s. 1 (6)) is one of the means by which a measure of equality is achieved between public corporations and the private sector. The N.E.B. is therefore bound by all statutes, its employees will not be civil servants, and *inter alia* the execution of judgments against the N.E.B. may be levied against its property, by either a seizure or sale in order to satisfy a judgment debt. [**24**]

The inclusion of the subsection however does not exclude or restrict the possibility of the N.E.B. acting as the agent of a Government department, either in the form specifically envisaged in s. 4 (overseas aid) or more broadly by undertaking an investigation into a firm or industry at the request of the Department of Industry. [25]

The National Enterprise Board will not be exempt from any tax, duty, rate levy or other charge, whether general or local (s. 1 (7)). But Stamp Duty is not chargeable on instruments executed for the purpose of the transfer to the Board of securities and property already held by the Crown (s. 5, Schd. 1, para. 18 (1)). This is another provision designed to ensure equality between public and private enterprises: if a holding company in the private sector reorganises its holdings no duty would be payable: it would normally be eligible for relief from conveyance or transfer duty. [26]

If a company is threatened by an undesirable foreign takeover, the share capital and specified assets of the threatened company may be vested in the Secretary of State or the N.E.B. (ss. 11–20). In this event no Stamp Duty is chargeable (Schd. 1, para. 18 (2)), thus following the precedent established in the Finance Act 1946 (A.L.S. Vol. 37) under which documents concerned with the vesting of property in nationalised industries are exempt from duty, when the industries are established. A vesting order can only be made if the Secretary of State is convinced, *inter alia*, that the national interest cannot be protected in any other way (s. 13 (3)). In other words, no British company is seeking to purchase the company threatened by undesirable foreign control. The exemption from Stamp Duty cannot, therefore, be interpreted as bestowing an unfair advantage on the N.E.B. at the expense of another company, for no such company exists. [27]

THE PURPOSES AND FUNCTIONS OF THE BOARD

The purposes for which the Board may exercise its functions are expressed in very vague and perhaps contradictory terms. This is not surprising and follows established precedent. It has become a commonplace to regard economic affairs as subject to violent and unpredictable changes of policy, presumably in response to changed circumstances, and it is doubtless considered appropriate for legislation in economic matters to accommodate such uncertainty. (It is apostasy to regard this attitude as a confusion between cause and effect.) An important consequence, however, is that the wording of s. 2 of the Industry Act 1975 imposes little discipline on the Board's activities and so it is virtually inconceivable that its *vires* could be exceeded, simply because they are drawn so loosely. An additional factor reinforcing the broadest possible interpretation of the Board's powers is the judicial reluctance to decide against the Executive's interpretation of legislation involving economic policy. In the past, judges have been less than enthusiastic in involving themselves in economic exegesis: this view is stated with clarity in *Charles Roberts & Co., Ltd.* v. *British Railways Board*, [1965] 1 WLR 396, at p. 400, *per* Ungoed-Thomas, J. "In general, judges are not qualified to decide questions of economic policy, and such questions are by their nature not justiciable." [28]

Arguably this reticence to review the activities of goverment and its agencies is especially important in a legal system in which no concept of "unfair competition" is recognised, and in which the intentional infliction of harm in the economic sphere is only remediable in a very narrow range of circumstances (*Mogul Steamship Co.* v. *McGregor Gow & Co.*, (1892) A.C. 25). It is a moot point whether the jejune legal provisions inserted into past nationalisation statutes, and the rather more powerful sanction of a ministerial direction, found in s. 7 of the Industry Act, are together effective discipline on the Executive's abuse of power. [**29**]

JURISDICTION

The three purposes of the N.E.B. are each specified to relate to the United Kingdom or any part of the United Kingdom. The five functions are expressed by s. 2 (3) to apply to the U.K. and "elsewhere" and the eight powers outlined in s. 2 (4) which are not exhaustive of the N.E.B.'s authority, have no geographical limit placed upon them. Two consequences follow from this. By expressing the N.E.B.'s authority in terms of the United Kingdom some uncertainty is created over the precise relationship and responsibilities of the N.E.B. and the Scottish Development Agency, the Welsh Development Agency and the Northern Ireland Finance Corporation. It is clear that the recently established Development Agencies are restricted in their activities to Scotland and Wales, but the role of the N.E.B. in Scotland and in Wales is nowhere defined in the principal Act. In the "Regeneration of British Industry", Cmnd. 5710 (1974), para. 72, we are told that the "appropriate functions" of the N.E.B. shall be carried out by the Development Agencies. But what are "appropriate functions" is not statutorily defined, and will be a matter of administration", not legislation. In the "Draft Guidelines" to the public conduct of the N.E.B. (at para. 31) it is stated that the N.E.B. will consult the Agencies before taking action on proposals affecting companies with significant interests in Scotland, Wales and Northern Ireland. It is expected that the Agencies themselves will take the initiative in dealing with companies which ". . . are wholly or predominately of concern to them but will consult the N.E.B. as necessary". Second, although the purposes of the N.E.B. are naturally styled to apply only to the United Kingdom this does not preclude the N.E.B. from acquiring assets abroad—for instance, the foreign assets held by a subsidiary of a company acquired in the United Kingdom—provided that the reasons for such an acquisition fall within the purposes specified in s. 2 (1) (*a*)–(*c*). *If* it can be proved that a purchase of foreign assets is motivated by reasons falling beyond the purposes specified in the Act, then the N.E.B. would be open to a specific ministerial directive preventing the acquisition. [**30**]

THE OBJECTIVES OF THE BOARD

The purposes of the N.E.B. are (i) the development or assistance of the economy of the United Kingdom or any part of the United Kingdom, (ii) the promotion in any part of the United Kingdom of industrial efficiency and international competitiveness and (iii) the provision maintenance and safeguarding of productive employment in any part of the United Kingdom (s. 2 (1)). [**31**]

These objectives clearly reflect the Government's conviction that industry has not carried out the social and economic obligations that the "national interest" would expect of it, namely a high level of investment particularly in areas of unemployment, a higher volume of exports and the expansion of employment opportunities, and that the N.E.B. should have as its object the securing of these social and economic objectives.   [**32**]

The wording bears a close resemblance to the form adopted in s. 2 (1) of the Industrial Reorganisation Act 1966 and s. 7 (1) (*a*) of the Industry Act 1972. An interesting omission, remembering the tenor of the White Paper which preceded the Industry Act 1975, "The Regeneration of British Industry", Cmnd. 5710 (1974), para. 1, is any reference to "profitability". Further, in the original bill, clause 2 (1) (*c*) was written with no reference to the provision . . . of "productive" employment. This led to the inevitable criticism that "efficiency" (s. 2 (1) (*b*)) was in conflict with the safeguarding of employment in industry, the more so if such industries were already overmanned or in decline.
[**33**]

The word "productive" was inserted by a House of Lords amendment (363 H.L. Deb. (1974–5), col. 100), presumably in order to make a distinction between "productive" and "unproductive" employment. The former should be provided, maintained and safeguarded, and the latter should not. It is, however, somewhat difficult to conceive of an extra employee contributing nothing to output: in the absence of the discarded market mechanism there are no unequivocal criteria to distinguish between the two categories of labour. The Government accepted the principle of a limit to the preservation of employment as an end in itself, but refused to make s. 2 (1) (*c*) subject to s. 2 (1) (*a*) and (*b*).

In general, the wording of s. 2 (1) is so vague that it would be extremely difficult to assess whether the objectives of the Board have ever been fulfilled. This remarkable and melancholy conclusion can have few counterparts in legislation pertaining to non-economic matters.   [**34**]

THE FUNCTIONS OF THE BOARD

Proceeding from the "purpose for which the Board may exercise their functions", to the "functions" themselves, the Board shall establish undertakings, promote the reorganisation of industry, extend public ownership into "profitable" areas of manufacturing industry, promote "industrial democracy" in Board holdings and take over and manage State owned securities and properties. The Board may do anything, whether in the United Kingdom or elsewhere, which is calculated to facilitate the discharge of the above functions, subject only to the capacity of the Board as a statutory corporation and the general law which governs such a corporation.   [**35**]

Section 2 (2) (*a*) states that the Board shall have the function of "establishing, maintaining or developing or promoting or assisting the establishment, maintenance or development of any industrial undertaking". "Industrial undertaking" is defined by reference to s. 37 (1), as any commercial activity, and is not necessarily confined to "manufacturing industry" as described in Orders III–XIX of the Standard Industrial Classification and s. 37 (3). Although it is clear that the main focus of the Board's activities will be manufacturing industry the Government felt it unwise to place a statutory restriction on the Board's influence; neither the I.R.C. nor the Department administering the Industry Act 1972 were so restricted. [**36**]

The freedom to establish new undertakings was sought in order to locate new State enterprises in areas of high unemployment. There has been growing dissatisfaction in recent years with the efficacy of regional incentives, and the Government felt it ought to play a more direct role in creating employment than hitherto. A close foreign parallel to the N.E.B., the Italian I.R.I., regards regional development as a major priority and an overwhelming proportion of its new investment is obliged by law to be deployed in areas of high unemployment or under-employment; I.R.I. was the subject of close scrutiny by the Trade and Industry Sub-Committee of the Expenditure Committee (Sixth Report "Public Money in the Private Sector", HC 347 of 1971–2). An added justification for the Board possessing this function is its use as a possible challenge to existing monopolists; the Board could establish an undertaking in competition with a private monopolist. [**37**]

The advent of the State as entrepreneur, that is, the promoter of new enterprises, rather than the owner of existing entities is bound to raise a number of interesting legal questions, among which the problem of "unfair competition" is the most immediate. When the State was content to take an *industry* into public ownership, questions of competition between public and private enterprise all but disappeared and were reduced to inter-industry competition and possibly to ensuring that any peripheral or ancillary activities owned by a State corporation competed on equal terms with the private sector. [**38**]

In the context of the Industry Act 1975 it was feared by the Parliamentary opposition that the State would discriminate in favour of N.E.B. established companies, within an industry, to the detriment of competitors. Such discrimination might take the form of improper preference in Government procurement, permitting privileged access to capital thus allowing the company to undercut competitors' prices and, lastly, the improper exercise of the Secretary of State's discretion to refer certain monopolies and all mergers to the Monopolies Commission. There are other examples of potential bias in the treatment of a State-owned and private concerns, reflecting in part the enormous discretion the Secretary of State possesses in economic life. In the Industry Act 1975 the only limitations on the Board's activities, short of a ministerial direction (s. 7) are, first, the duty placed on the Board to earn an "adequate" return on capital (s. 6 (3), to be discussed later) and, second, the general rules surrounding fair trading, from which the Board, as a statutory corporation, is not exempt, but which have only limited application to the situation where an aggrieved competitor faces "unfair competition". The United Kingdom's membership of the European Communities places constraints upon the comportment of undertakings over which the State exercises control (E.E.C. Treaty, art. 90 (1), and E.C.S.C. Treaty, art. 60; see Case 109/75R, *National Carbonising Co., Ltd.* v. *E.C. Commission and National Coal Board*, [1975] 2 C.M.L.R. 457, O.J. 1976 L35/6). The problem is further confounded if the N.E.B. proposes to establish companies in competition to existing monopolies. The *raison d'être* of such a policy is the removal of some of the "evils" associated with monopoly, primarily the typically "excessive" differential between prices and costs. But when would such competitive price-cutting become an abuse of the N.E.B.'s power? In any event, the Government possess the power, not only to order the reduction of prices following a Monopolies Commission inquiry but to order divestiture, that is the creation of two or more concerns from the original monopolist (Fair Trading Act 1973, Sch. 3, Part 2, A.L.S. Vol. 229).   [**39**]

The Board's second function is the "promoting or assisting the reorganisation or development of an industry or any undertaking in an industry" (s. 2 (2) (*b*)). This function bears a very close parallel with the merger broking activities of the I.R.C. already remarked upon, though the I.R.C. Act 1966, s. 2 (1) (*a*), did not extend to ". . . any undertaking in an industry . . ." it was thought desirable for the N.E.B. to have the power to take an interest in a particular firm within an industry.   [**40**]

THE EXTENSION OF PUBLIC OWNERSHIP

The Board's third function is the highly controversial and idiosyncratic one of "extending public ownership into profitable areas of manufacturing industry" (s. 2 (2) (*c*)). It is controversial because it brings into relief the cleavage between the two major parties regarding public enterprise. On one side lies the Conservative Opposition, anxious to restrict public ownership to a narrow range of industries and to limit the form of any public assistance which it is obliged to dispense to loans and guarantees—and then only to companies which are in manifestly temporary difficulties. And on the other side stands the sponsoring Government, regarding public ownership or participation as a means by which individual companies are forced to conduct their affairs more in accordance with the Government's interpretation of the national interest, and, equally, anxious to move public enterprise into expanding and profitable sectors. It was not surprising, therefore, that s. 2 (2) (*c*) should have engendered so much hostility and that the House of Lords should pass an amendment removing it from the Bill altogether. Its inclusion is idiosyncratic, however, because there is nothing in s. 2 (2) (*a*) (*b*) and perhaps (*d*) to prevent the Board taking a shareholding in a company: the Board may "do anything . . . calculated to discharge the functions specified in s. 2 (2) . . . including the acquisition of securities" (s. 2 (3), (4) (*a*)) provided that the Board's legal obligations are fulfilled (s. 2 (5)). Further, by similar reasoning, there is nothing to prevent the Board taking interests in "manufacturing" or indeed any other sector (particularly banking), or that the enterprise should be "profitable" as opposed to "unprofitable". For completeness, the word "areas" seems to have defied interpretation: it is legally meaningless.   [**41**]

The philosophy behind this central part of the Act is to ensure that the Government has more direct authority over certain companies than it would have if it deployed ". . . old and well respected methods of Keynesian demand management", that is, by controlling the environment in which businesses operate. The Government is seized of the view that certain very substantial companies have sufficient domination over markets, both nationally and internationally, that only direct involvement with individual concerns will have the results desired by the Government. Planning Agreements, to be discussed below, are born of the same belief.   [**42**]

A natural difficulty is the problem of reconciling the N.E.B.'s desires as a shareholder with shareholders' commercial interests. It is not difficult to envisage situations where the N.E.B.'s interests might conflict with the interests of other shareholders, for instance, in the maintenance of a loss-making plant to preserve employment. It is likely, therefore, that N.E.B. shareholdings will, wherever possible, be exclusive holdings, simply to avoid the possibility of an action by an aggrieved minority shareholder. (A simpler and cheaper expedient would have been to propose an amendment to the Companies Acts insisting that every company should include in its memorandum and articles of association a provision that the company should operate in the "national interest". This would, however, leave the interpretation of the "national interest" to the judiciary.) Where a total shareholding is impossible past practice indicates that the Government or the N.E.B. will acquire more than 10% of the share capital, in order to avoid the possibility of falling foul of the provisions of s. 209 of the Companies Act 1948. [**43**]

It is envisaged that public ownership will be extended by means of the acquisition of shares. Unlike the provisions found in the Industrial Expansion Act 1968 and the Industry Act 1972 there is no stipulation that the company's consent is required. Acquisition will be the product of a private bargain between the N.E.B. and a willing seller, irrespective of the views of the company's board. The "Guidelines" suggest a limit on the power of the N.E.B.: the Board shall not acquire more than 10% by nominal value of the shares carrying unrestricted voting rights in a publicly quoted company without the consent of the directors of that company, unless it informs the Secretary of State what size of holding it would like to secure eventually. The Board will be free to proceed if, after a reasonable period, the Secretary of State has not indicated to the contrary (Sch. 1, para. 8). In addition, s. 209 of the Companies Act 1948 (the power to acquire shares of shareholders dissenting from a scheme or contract approved by the majority) shall have effect in relation to the transfer of shares in a company to the N.E.B. (Sch. 1, para. 19). [**44**]

LIMITS ON THE BOARD'S POWER TO ACQUIRE SHARE CAPITAL

The N.E.B. or any of its subsidiaries (as defined in the Companies Act 1948, s. 154 (11 and 12 Geo. 6, c. 38), or the Companies Act (N.I.) 1960, s. 148) *cannot* acquire any of the share capital of a company except with the consent of the Secretary of State, or in accordance with any general authority given by the Secretary of State, if

(a) the acquisition would take the N.E.B. or N.E.B.'s subsidiaries holding, to 30% or more of the voting shares of the company, *or*
(b) the total value of the N.E.B. or subsidiary's holding, at acquisition, was more than £10m (s. 10 (1)), subject to the provision found in "Guidelines" (para. 8) which indicates that the Secretary of State proposes to give a statutory general authority under which subsidiaries of the N.E.B. may acquire 30% or more of the share capital in a company providing the acquisition is not opposed by the company and the cost of the total shareholding in the company does not exceed £500,000. [**45**]

These provisions apply to the Board and to all its subsidiaries and are not confined to those subsidiaries which are wholly owned, notwithstanding any inhibiting effect this may have on joint ventures. In addition, it is clearly the purpose of the section to embrace not only the acquisition of *existing* share capital, but also to include voting shares issued to the Board or any subsidiary. It is expressly stated that shares which possess restricted voting rights at any general meeting of the company should not be counted in calculating the Board or subsidiary's total shareholding (s. 10 (2) (4)). Loan stock, convertible or otherwise, and warrants are not to be included as components of share capital for the purposes of s. 10 (1) (*a*), a practice followed by the City Code on Take-overs and Mergers. But, if convertible loan stock is converted into equity, there is a corresponding addition to the share capital. The act of conversion, it is submitted, must be regarded as an acquisition by the Board or subsidiary, and if as a result, the 30% threshhold is reached or exceeded, the Secretary of State's consent would be required. The limit of 30% was chosen advisedly in order not to conflict with the City Code on Takeovers and Mergers. The Code has no statutory effect, but the Government gave frequent undertakings in Com-mittee and in the "Guidelines" (para. 6) that its provisions would be observed. A query remains, however, over the status of preference shares which acquire voting rights if a dividend has been passed. It is thought likely that s. 10 (2) (4) is designed with such a situation in mind. But in view of the responsibilities that the N.E.B. is likely to assume such an interpretation presents a loophole in the qualifications for ministerial approval, more striking in view of the absence of direct Parliamentary approval of each acquisition. The provisions of s. 10 (3) make clear that where the N.E.B. already holds share capital with restricted rights it is to be disregarded for the purpose of determining whether the 30% rule applies.   [**46**]

Section 10 (1) (*b*) covers not only equity shareholdings but also preference shares and it is designed to limit the amount of risk capital which the N.E.B. may put into a company without the Secretary of State's consent.   [**47**]

The specified figure of £10m. may be compared with that of £5m. in s. 64 (1) (*b*) of the Fair Trading Act, 1973, which is the limit for assets taken over above which a merger may be referred to the Monopolies Commission by the Secretary of State. In a merger situation to which ss. 62–68 of the Fair Trading Act 1973 apply, the Secretary of State may refer the bid to the Monopolies Commission, but it seems unlikely that communications between the Secretary of State for Industry and the Secretary of State for Prices and Consumer Protection should be so poor as to permit this to happen. (In his evidence to the Trade and Industry Sub-Committee of the Expenditure Committee, Q.1278 (*ante*), Sir Arnold Weinstock remarked that the principal contribution of the I.R.C. to the G.E.C. takeover of A.E.I. was that it ". . . removed any obstacles that Government might have put in the way such as reference to the Monopolies Commission. . . .") In fact, the "Guidelines" specify that the N.E.B. must consult with the Director-General of Fair Trading before involving itself in any activity qualifying for reference to the Monopolies and Mergers Commission (para. 9).   [**48**]

Section 10 (4) permits the N.E.B. to establish new bodies corporate without the limitations found in the rest of the section. Without such a provision the

N.E.B. would be required to obtain the Secretary of State's approval to form a new wholly owned subsidiary. It is clear though, that the N.E.B. could participate in a joint venture company without the Secretary of State's approval, provided the N.E.B. itself formed the joint venture company. The Board is permitted to engage in joint ventures within a limit of £25m. for each project; beyond this figure the consent of the Secretary of State is required. In all cases he should be given advance notice of its intentions ("Guidelines", para. 11).

[49]

THE PROMOTION OF INDUSTRIAL DEMOCRACY

It is a function of the N.E.B. that it will promote industrial democracy in undertakings which the Board controls (s. 2 (2) (*d*)). This aim mirrors the phrasing of "The Regeneration of British Industry" at para. 26, ". . . the N.E.B. will play its part in ensuring that enterprises under its control provide for the full involvement of employees in decision-making at all levels". The Government resisted backbench Committee pressure to include in the Bill a general power to promote industrial democracy in all companies, not merely those owned by the N.E.B. This was forestalled, and indeed a Private Member's Bill withdrawn (Industrial Democracy Bill, HC Bill 60 of 1975) by the formation of a Committee under the chairmanship of Lord Bullock empowered to examine the most appropriate means by which formal industrial democracy should be introduced in Britain. [50]

TAKING OVER PUBLICLY OWNED SECURITIES

The last function of the N.E.B. is the taking over of publicly owned securities and other publicly owned property, and holding and managing securities and property which are taken over (s. 2 (2) (*e*)). This provision permits the N.E.B. to take over shareholdings already held for the benefit of the Crown and any which may be acquired in the future. "Publicly owned" is defined in s. 37 (4) as securities and other property held "(a) by or on behalf of the Crown; (b) by a company all of whose shares are held by or on behalf of the Crown or by a wholly owned subsidiary of such a company; (c) by any corporation constituted by or under any enactment under which an industry or part of an industry is carried on by that corporation under national ownership or control; or (d) by a wholly owned subsidiary of any such corporation". If the Government wished, therefore, all or part of the assets of a nationalised industry could be transferred to the N.E.B. [51]

THE POWERS OF THE BOARD

The N.E.B. may do anything, whether in the United Kingdom or elsewhere, which is calculated to facilitate the discharge of the functions specified in s. 2 (2) or is incidental or conducive to their discharge (s. 2 (3)). Such a provision is standard form in statutes establishing public corporations. The implications are spelt out in s. 2 (4) though the examples provided are not exhaustive. The powers are, of course, only exercisable in so far as they contribute to the purposes and functions of the N.E.B., already discussed. [52]

The Board has power:

"(a) to acquire, hold and dispose of securities". This power is essential in view of the functions specified in s. 2 (2) (*a*)–(*c*), and although the N.E.B. proposes to build up and retain a portfolio of shareholdings it will occasionally wish to dispose of holdings (see IRC Act 1966, s. 2 (3) (*a*)). This right of disposal is qualified, however, by the need for the Secretary of State's consent for the disposal of voting shares held by the Board or its subsidiaries, except where the total value of the disposal does not exceed £500,000 ("Guidelines", para. 1).

"(b) to form bodies corporate" (see para. [**49**] *ante*).

"(c) to form partnerships with other persons".

"(d) to make loans." The White Paper made it clear that the N.E.B. will be a new source of capital for manufacturing industry (para. 24).

"(e) to guarantee obligations (arising out of loans or otherwise) incurred by other persons". It may be more efficient, and cheaper, for the N.E.B. to guarantee private borrowings or other obligations rather than provide funds directly (I.R.C. Act 1966, s. 2 (3) (*c*)).

"(f) to acquire and dispose of land, premises, plant, machinery and equipment".

"(g) to make land, premises, plant, machinery and equipment available for use by other persons".

"(h) to provide services in relation to finance, management administration or organisation of industry". [**53**]

OVERSEAS AID

As an extension to the power last mentioned, an amendment was introduced in the House of Lords (365 H.L. Deb. (1974–5), col. 205) at the request of the Minister of Overseas Development empowering the N.E.B. to provide technical assistance to a developing country. The section embraces two situations, the first of which is where the N.E.B. and the Minister for Overseas Development enter into an agreement for technical assistance to be provided as part of the official British overseas aid programme. The Secretary of State for Industry's consent is required, and the costs would be met from the overseas aid programme. The second situation provides for a direct agreement between the N.E.B. and the Government of the developing country, or with another appropriate body, which would not form part of the aid programme but for which the N.E.B. would be reimbursed directly by the Government or organisation assisted. In this latter case, the consent of both the Secretary of State and the Minister of Overseas Development is required. It is unlikely that these powers will ever assume great importance, in the work of the N.E.B.: in the longer run, the N.E.B.'s principal contribution will be the release of staff for assignments in developing countries. [**54**]

TRANSFER OF PUBLICLY OWNED PROPERTY TO THE BOARD

Paragraph 29 of the White Paper sets out certain existing government shareholdings, which, it is intended, will be vested in the N.E.B. These shareholdings were acquired under a number of different statutory authorities, e.g. Rolls-Royce (1971) Ltd. by virtue of the Rolls-Royce Purchase Act 1971, International Computers (Holdings) Ltd. under the Industrial Expansion Act 1968, and in none of which was it contemplated that the property would be transferred to an agency such as the N.E.B. Section 5 ensures that nothing in the Act or in any current or future legislation (subject to an express provision to the contrary) shall prevent the transfer to the N.E.B. or the Board's nominees of any publicly owned securities or other publicly owned property. The section includes, therefore, not only the holdings specified in the White Paper but all present and future Government shareholdings. "Publicly owned" (see para. [51], *ante*) expressly includes nationalised industries and in future it is possible that certain assets of nationalised industries would be judged to be managed more efficiently by N.E.B. The section provides the necessary authority for the industries in question to dispose of their assets to the Board. In addition, there are two specific situations where the Secretary of State may acquire securities and other property and may subsequently wish to transfer them to the Board. The first relates to the exercise of the powers derived from ss. 7 and 8 of the Industry Act 1972 (i.e. where the exercise of such powers has not been delegated to the N.E.B. by virtue of s. 3, *post*). The second situation refers to the compulsory acquisition of undertakings by virtue of a vesting order (see ss. 11–20, *post*). Where such assets are originally vested in the Secretary of State they may be transferred to the Board. The use of the phrase "securities or other property" permits the transfer of assets of a body corporate rather than equity: in certain circumstances it may be desirable to vest assets rather than shares. [55]

The Act provides that no publicly owned security or property shall be transferred without the consent of the Secretary of State or in the absence of any general authority given by the Secretary of State (s. 5 (2)). A copy of such general authority must be laid before each House of Parliament. Further Parliamentary accountability is ensured by the provisions of s. 5 (4): if the Secretary of State has consented to the transfer and if the consideration is determined at more than £1m., the Secretary of State must lay before each House of Parliament a statement specifying: (i) the securities or other property to be transferred; (ii) the transferor; (iii) the consideration, and (iv) the date of consent. If there is a delay in arriving at a satisfactory valuation and the consideration is likely to be more than £1m. the Secretary of State must proceed to supply Parliament with the details specified in s. 5 (4) and should lay before each House a statement specifying the consideration for the transfer ". . . as soon as practicable after its amount has been determined" (s. 5 (6)). [56]

FINANCIAL DUTIES OF THE BOARD

The Secretary of State has to determine the financial duties of the N.E.B., after consultation with the Board and with the approval of the Treasury (s. 6). Different determinations may be made for different assets and activities of the Board: this has been judged necessary because of the wide range of the N.E.B.'s activities and it was thought appropriate to distinguish between investments in profitable industry and investments made in order to promote reorganisations, the benefits of which may not be immediately reflected in a balance sheet, if at all. In taking investment decisions though, the Board is enjoined to have regard to the profitability of the projects concerned. In addition, separate determinations were judged necessary in order to distinguish between assets which the N.E.B. is obliged to acquire following a direction of the Secretary of State (under the powers contained in ss. 3, 11–20 and, generally, s. 7) and those assets which were acquired on the Board's initiative.   [57]

A duty is imposed on the Secretary of State and the Treasury before making a determination, to satisfy themselves that the duties imposed on the Board are *likely, taken together* to result in an *adequate* return on capital employed by the Board (s. 6 (3)). This is somewhat Delphic. As remarked earlier there are few guarantees ensuring that competition between the N.E.B. and other concerns will be "fair" (see para. [38], *ante*) and throughout the passage of the Bill the Government relied repeatedly upon the financial discipline imposed by s. 6 to act as a check on non-commercial behaviour on the part of the Board. (The "Guidelines" insist that the Board will avoid showing "undue preference" in its trading relationships, (para. 16) which, though useful, does not provide a remedy for an aggrieved trader.) The financial disciplines imposed upon the Board have a significance which goes beyond the curtailment of public pro-fligacy and therefore deserve close scrutiny.   [58]

A determination is a matter solely between the Secretary of State and the Treasury (or in the words of Mr. Fairbairn, M.P., during the Committee stage of the Bill, that ". . . frightful brontosaurus . . . scornful, difficult, inept and despicable . . ."). The phrase ". . . likely, taken together, to result in an adequate return on capital employed by the Board" is replete with uncertainty. "Likely" connotes a debatable state of affairs (which, nevertheless, is not to be debated). "Taken together", implies that certain activities should subsidise less profitable expenditure. This is contrary to recent practice that public enterprises should, as far as possible, be self-supporting, and any required subsidy should be specifically calculated and accounted for as such. Whatever the extent of cross-subsidisation in the private sector whenever it has been discovered in the course of inquiries, such as those undertaken by the Monopolies and Mergers Commission, it has normally been criticised as leading to a misallocation of resources. (A recent example is to be found in the Commission's report on the supply of contraceptive sheaths in the United Kingdom (HC135 of 1974–5, para. 209). Here a monopolist attempted unsuccessfully to justify high profits on the ground that it permitted the company to diversify.) "An adequate return" is a term unknown to similar statutes, and its interpretation is left to unreviewable discretion of the Secretary of State and the Treasury. Further-more, there is no reference in the Act to the time period in which this "adequate" return is "likely" to be earned.   [59]

Notwithstanding the wish to impose comparable financial disciplines to private concerns it was thought appropriate that the N.E.B. should not be subject to fundamentally different financial determinations than other nationa-lised concerns. Most nationalised industries have a statutory duty to break-even taking one year with another. Where public dividend capital is employed more specific financial duties must be provided in statutory form (see Iron and Steel Act 1969, s. 5). This is because interest on conventional loan capital is a charge against revenue before the calculation of profit, whereas dividends on public dividend capital are appropriations from profits. A break-even statutory duty would therefore be less burdensome on a body like the N.E.B., with a proportion of public dividend capital, than on other nationalised industries whose capital is all in the form of interest-bearing loans. The precedents of the Iron and Steel Act 1969 and other more recent legislation specify that the financial objective should be expressed in terms of rate of return on net assets (although this form can be amended and a different basis substituted by Statutory Instrument). As far as the N.E.B. is concerned it was thought inappropriate to insist that the financial duty should take the form of a minimum rate of return on *net* assets, particularly where subsidiaries are acquired at a price which differs from the net asset value. The form adopted permits flexibility in the criteria to be adopted from case to case, and will equally ensure that the return is related to the funds invested by the N.E.B. rather than the asset value it controls. [**60**]

A determination may relate to a period beginning before the date on which it is made and may include incidental or supplementary provisions (s. 6 (4)).

[**61**]

MINISTERIAL DIRECTIONS

The Secretary of State has the power, after consultation with the Board, to give the Board general or specific directions on the exercise of its functions as expressed in s. 2 (2) (s. 7 (1)) and the Board is required to give effect to any such direction, whether it is in agreement or not. The power to give directions of a general character in relation to the conduct of public corporations is a familiar one. (A complete list of statutes establishing public corporations in which a power of direction is included will be found in J. F. Garner's *Administrative Law*, 4th edn. 1974, Butterworths, Appendix to Chapter 10.) It is designed to enable the Government ". . . to influence the activities of the Board and its constituent companies in the national interest . . ." A "specific" direction is unusual: it was granted in the Atomic Energy Authority Act 1954, s. 3, but it could only be exercised when, in the opinion of the Lord President of the Council, overriding national interests so required. A similar power was inserted in the Civil Aviation Act 1971, s. 4 (3), but it was restricted to a number of specified purposes. A directly comparable provision to that contained in the present Act is to be found in s. 4 of the Petroleum and Submarine Pipe-line Act 1975. [**62**]

The perennial problem is to reconcile the possession of the power to direct the management of a public enterprise with the commercial and operating freedom of the management. The accumulated evidence seems to suggest that past experience has been far from happy and though there have been remarkably few formal directions there is evidence of informal and covert pressures upon the management of public corporations. The advent of a power of specific direction (as recommended by the First Report from the Select Committee on Nationalised Industries, Session 1967–8, HC 371–I of 1967–8, Vol. I, para. 649) has eliminated the semantic consideration of what contributes a "general" direction and will, it is intended, formalise the relationship between the Government and the Board, and obviate the necessity for private coercion. It is not intended to use the power of specific direction to intervene in day to day affairs. Moreover, s. 7 (3) instructs the Secretary of State to lay a copy of the direction (general or specific) before each House of Parliament within 28 days, or later provided that the delay is explained. And further, the Board's report for any accounting year must include any direction given under s. 7 during that year (s. 7 (4) and Sch. 2, para. 8 (4)).   [**63**]

LIMITS ON THE BOARD'S POWERS—THE MEDIA

Following an assurance given by the Government in Committee (Standing Committee E, 25 March 1975, col. 1408) formal restraints have been placed upon the Board's power to acquire direct or indirect interests in newspapers or broadcasting (infelicitously termed "media") (s. 9). Apart from any "house journal" which may emerge from within the N.E.B., neither the Board nor any of the Board's subsidiaries has the power to establish or acquire a shareholding in any undertaking the business of which is substantially the publishing of newspapers, magazines or periodicals for sale to the public in the United Kingdom. In addition, the Board or any of its subsidiaries cannot enter into any contract with the Independent Broadcasting Authority for the provision of programmes, nor can any shareholding or interest be acquired in any company the activities of which are substantially those of a programme contractor (as defined by s. 2 (3) of the Independent Broadcasting Authority Act 1973).
[**64**]

If the Board or any of its subsidiaries acquires any of the share capital of a company which carries on or has a direct or indirect interest in the business of publishing newspapers, magazines and periodicals, the Board has a duty to exercise its voting power to ensure that the business or interest in the business is disposed of as soon as practicable. Similarly, if a shareholding in a programme contractor is acquired the Board is under a duty to consult the Independent Broadcasting Authority as to what steps it should take with regard to the share capital and obey any direction given by the I.B.A.   [**65**]

The foregoing, however, does not prevent the acquisition of share capital by the Board or any of its subsidiaries if the acquisition is made under the powers found in ss. 7 and 8 of the Industry Act 1972 and delegated to the Board under s. 3 of the Industry Act 1975 (*post*). In addition, the Secretary of State may direct that the Board's duty of disposal of any interest in publishing should be suspended for a temporary period, but only if the disposal would result in serious commercial injury to the newspaper, magazine or periodical concerned.
[**66**]

Lastly, as a further restraint on the possible manipulation of the press by a Government agency, the N.E.B. and any of its subsidiaries is restricted in the exercise of its powers of control and influence over a newspaper, periodical or magazine or over the activities of a programme contractor, to financial and commercial matters only. It has no power to intervene in "editorial" matters and must make appropriate arrangements, to the satisfaction of the Secretary of State, that it has no responsibility for, or influence on, editorial functions (s. 9 (10); "Guidelines", para. 34).   [**67**]

FINANCIAL LIMITS ON THE BOARD'S POWERS

The N.E.B. has been endowed with an initial tranche of £700m. and a further £300m. will be made available by order of the Secretary of State, subject to the approval of the House of Commons. This sum will represent a charge on the Exchequer additional to that already authorised by other legislation, in particular, by s. 8 (6) and (7) of the Industry Act 1972. This Act originally limited sums paid and liabilities under any guarantees given, to £150m, which could be increased on not more than four occasions by tranches of up to £100m. The current charge is £350m (see the Financial Assistance for Industry (Increase of Limit) (No. 2) Order 1976, S.I. 1976 No. 155). In addition, the value of property transferred to the Board under s. 13 (2) will not count against the limit.   [68]

The four separate elements in the Board's finances are brought within the statutory limit. In each instance reference is made solely to the principal outstanding, not to any interest payable.

(a) The Board's "general external borrowing", including that of wholly owned subsidiaries. "General external borrowing" is defined by s. 8 (4) to embrace all borrowing by the Board and wholly owned subsidiaries, except in the following four situations: (i) sums loaned to the Board by a wholly owned subsidiary; (ii) sums issued by the Treasury to fulfil a guarantee on borrowing by the Board (such a sum is already included in the limits by virtue of s. 8 (1) (*b*)); (iii) sums given or lent to the Board for the purposes of exercising the powers of ss. 7 and 8 of the Industry Act 1972. Assistance under s. 8, as earlier noted, is limited to £350m, and money loaned to the N.E.B. will count against this limit. There are no limits to the amount of money which may be disbursed under s. 7; (iv) borrowing by wholly owned subsidiaries from the Board or from other wholly owned subsidiaries. Schedule 2, para. 3 provides that all other borrowing by wholly owned subsidiaries must be agreed by the Secretary of State and approved by the Treasury (s. 8 (4)).

(b) Sums issued by the Treasury in order to fulfil Treasury guarantees offered on borrowings by the Board, and not repaid to the Treasury. The authority for such guarantees, the conditions under which they are to be made, and repaid, are found in Sch. 2, para. 4 (s. 8 (1) (*b*)).

(c) Sums invested in the Board by the Government as "public dividend capital", under Sch. 2, para. 5 (1). Not all the public dividend capital will count against the limit, however, for the Secretary of State may direct that part of the Board's capital should be excluded and treated as debt, owed to the Secretary of State in respect of property initially vested in the Board or subsequently transferred to it by the Crown (Sch. 2, paras. 5 (2) and 6). This includes the value of assets acquired in accordance with a direction under s. 3 or vested in the Board under s. 13. In none of these cases will the Board be drawing upon the resources limited in s. 8 (2) and so the value of the assets acquired does not count against the financial limits.

(d) If the Board guarantees a loan, under s. 2 (4) (*c*), a contingent liability falls upon the Exchequer: the guarantee is included in the limit specified.   [69]

In the first instance the limit specified is £700m, but the Secretary of State may, by order, with the consent of the Treasury and following a resolution of the House of Commons, raise the limit to £1,000m.   [70]

THE GOVERNMENT AND THE BOARD

The Government proposes to oversee the activities of the N.E.B. by formally requesting the Board to furnish the Department of Industry with a Corporate Plan, which will be revised annually, setting out its strategy for the following years. It is envisaged that this will provide the framework for discussions regarding the N.E.B.'s objectives. Among the topics to be considered are, the financial returns sought, investment and the proportion of investment in the assisted areas, improvements in efficiency and exports. In addition, and as part of the Corporate Plan, the N.E.B. must provide annually an investment and financing programme, covering the period of the Public Expenditure Survey, for consideration by the Department and the Treasury. This annual review will be divided into parts relating to:

(a) existing large N.E.B. holdings;
(b) acquisitions, joint ventures and new ventures;
(c) assistance operations;

with a discussion of the balance between them. These discussions will enable the Department in consultation with the Treasury, to set a ceiling to the amount of Government funds—whether by way of advances from the National Loan Funds (N.L.F.) or Public Dividend Capital (P.D.C.), which the N.E.B. should receive during the coming year. Within this limit sums will be advanced on evidence of proof of need for the N.E.B's business purposes. For day to day finance the N.E.B. will be authorised to make overdraft arrangements with its bankers in accordance with the provisions of Sch. 2. In addition, after allowing for interest on borrowings from the N.L.F. and dividend payments on P.D.C., the N.E.B. may retain its profits for reinvestment.   [71]

PARLIAMENTARY CONTROL OF THE BOARD

A number of situations arise under the Act where the Secretary of State must seek Parliamentary approval before proceeding to a particular course of action. When the N.E.B. assists companies following a direction under s. 3 the funds so applied will be a charge on Departmental Votes. The Public Accounts Committee (P.A.C.) will therefore be able to question the Accounting Officer of the Department of Industry in order to satisfy itself that the N.E.B. has adequate arrangements for monitoring the financial assistance provided to companies under direction. A Treasury minute dated 14 August 1872 states that the Accounting Officer, ". . . signs the Appropriation Account and thereby makes himself responsible for its correctness . . . It cannot be too distinctly announced that responsibility for the proper conduct of financial business cannot be delegated to the subordinate officers who may be placed in charge." But for all other functions which the N.E.B. may discharge, there is no Parliamentary scrutiny comparable to that of the P.A.C. It has been suggested that the Select Committee on the Nationalised Industries should superintend the activities of the N.E.B., but to date, nothing has come of this.   [72]

CHAPTER 3

SELECTIVE FINANCIAL ASSISTANCE TO INDUSTRY

By virtue of ss. 7 and 8 of the Industry Act 1972 the Secretary of State has acquired wide powers of selective financial intervention in industry. He can provide financial assistance in virtually any form and in virtually any circumstance. Since 1972 there has been a steady growth in the use of such powers accompanied by the contraction of payments under the superseded provisions of the Local Employment Act 1972. In part, this represents a further example of the more specific approach to Government intervention in the affairs of industry by the State referred to in Chapter 1. **[73]**

The Industry Act 1975 substantially amends the earlier Act and, in addition, it empowers the Secretary of State to delegate his responsibility for selective financial intervention to the National Enterprise Board—placing a corresponding duty on the Board to comply with any direction. **[74]**

INDUSTRY ACT 1972, S. 7

Under s. 7 of the Industry Act 1972 the Secretary of State, with the consent of the Treasury, is authorised to provide financial assistance for undertakings which are wholly or mainly in the "assisted areas". He may do this where, in his opinion, the assistance is ". . . likely to provide, maintain or safeguard employment in those areas" (Industry Act 1972, s. 7 (1)). Financial assistance may be given on ". . . any terms or conditions and by any description of investment or lending or guarantee, or by making grants" (s. 7 (3)) for the following purposes set out in s. 7 (2), which are:

(a) to promote the development or modernisation of an industry;
(b) to promote the efficiency of an industry;
(c) to create, expand or sustain productive capacity in an industry, or in undertakings in an industry;
(d) to promote the reconstruction, reorganisation or conversion of an industry or of undertakings in an industry;
(e) to encourage the growth of, or the proper distribution of undertakings in, an industry;
(f) to encourage arrangements for ensuring that any contraction of an industry proceeds in an orderly way.

To a very large extent the Act is administered locally. Applications for assistance involving sums of up to £1m must be made to the Department of Industry's offices in Scotland, Wales, the Northern, Yorkshire, Humberside and North Western regions, who provided that the application fell within certain "guidelines" (see Industry Act Annual Report, Appendix D, HC 620 of 1974–5) will deal with the matter without reference to London. The regional offices, may however, refer the application to regional, non-statutory Industrial Development Boards for advice. **[75]**

From 1st July 1975 ministerial responsibility for regional selective assistance in Scotland and Wales has fallen upon the Secretaries of State for Scotland and Wales respectively (HC WA (1974–5) 883 c 712–713). But responsibility for cases in England and "for certain projects with implications for the whole of Great Britain", remains with the Secretary of State for Industry. **[76]**

General "guidelines" for regional selective assistance have been published, and supplement detailed operating rules within the Department of Industry, which have not been made public. Broadly, the purpose in providing assistance under s. 7 is to encourage and safeguard employment. Projects qualifying for assistance fall into two categories: (a) new projects and expansions which create additional employment; and (b) projects, which do not provide extra jobs but preserve existing ones (e.g. modernisation or rationalisation schemes). Situations falling beyond these two categories are decided on their own merits. There is great flexibility in the forms of assistance offered but the method adopted will largely depend on the category of the proposed project. **[77]**

Projects which create employment may qualify for one or more of five forms of aid:

(i) Loans at concessionary rates towards any of the normal capital requirements, including working capital, of an undertaking. The concessionary rate is somewhat lower than commercial interest levels and is currently $8\frac{1}{2}\%$.

(ii) Interest Relief Grants—which, as an alternative to a loan at the concessionary level, may be granted for moneys obtained from commercial sources or by self-financing. An interest relief grant permits the supplicant company to seek funds from private sources and is the subsidy equivalent of a concessionary loan. But it places less stress on public expenditure and also avoids the full vetting procedure which is needed to safeguard public money when a loan is given.

(iii) Financial assistance may also be provided in the form of share capital ". . . in appropriate cases". Although shares or stock cannot be acquired without the company's consent (Industry Act 1972, s. 7 (4), in contrast to the absence of such a requirement in the Industry Act of 1975), provisions limiting the acquisition of loan and share capital to those situations where in the opinion of the Secretary of State the assistance cannot or cannot appropriately be given in any other way, have been repealed. In addition, the requirement that such interests must be disposed of as soon as is reasonably practicable has been dispensed with (Sch. 4, para. 1 (a), s. 22). The combined effect of the two amendments to s. 7 (5) of the Industry Act 1972 enables the Secretary of State to take and keep a shareholding in a company appropriate to the assistance he is making available, providing only that the company consents.

(iv) Where an undertaking moves into an assisted area from a location outside an assisted area a grant of 80% of the "reasonable costs" of the removal of plant, machinery, stocks, materials and the employer's net statutory redundancy payments at the old location, will be paid subject to the Department of Industry's discretion.

(v) Where an undertaking moves into an assisted area from a location outside any assisted area and that undertaking is classified under Orders XXII–XXVII of the Standard Industrial Classification (broadly, service enterprises), plus other company offices and research and development units, it may receive, in addition to any other form of assistance, a Service Industry Removal Grant, amounting to (a) a fixed grant of £800 for each employee moved up to a limit of 50% of the number of additional jobs created in the assisted area; and (b) a grant to cover approved rent of the premises for up to three years in an Intermediate Area and up to five years in a Development Area. Equivalent help may be given if premises are bought rather than rented.   [**78**]

Projects which encourage modernisation and rationalisation, but do not create additional jobs, are only assisted where finance cannot be obtained from commercial sources. Loans are granted at approximately commercial rates though assistance may be given in the form of share capital. Assistance is limited to manufacturing, construction and mining and to projects in service industries which have a genuine choice of location between assisted areas and the rest of the country.   [**79**]

It should be emphasised that the foregoing is a précis of published administrative rules and inferences from observed practice. The Secretary of State has complete discretion in designating an area as "assisted" (Industry Act 1972, s. 1 (4) (5)) defined for the purposes of s. 7 as special development areas, development areas and intermediate areas (Industry Act 1972, s. 7 (7)). Designation or redesignation is made by a statutory instrument: see the Special Development Areas Order 1972; S.I. 1972 No. 1234; the Assisted Areas Order 1974, S.I. 1974 No. 1372.   [**80**]

INDUSTRY ACT 1972, S. 8

Section 8 deals with the provision of financial assistance both within and outside the assisted areas. The purposes are the same as those expressed in s. 7 (2) but instead of a justification based upon the employment effect of the aid it must ". . . benefit the economy of the United Kingdom or any part of the United Kingdom and it is in the national interest that the financial assistance should be provided on the scale and in the form and manner proposed".   [**81**]

Certain qualifications to s. 8 powers have been swept away by s. 22 of the Industry Act 1975. They are:

(i) that financial assistance can be provided only where, in the Secretary of State's opinion, it cannot, or cannot appropriately, be provided otherwise than by him (s. 8 (1) (c), now repealed). The Industrial Development Advisory Board, in its report on the year ending 31st March 1974, drew attention to the few applications made by individual companies under s. 8 and suggested that one of the reasons for its infrequent use was the need to satisfy s. 8 (1) (c). No comparable restriction has ever applied to s. 7 of the Industry Act 1972, and in deleting this restriction, the Government is seeking to encourage greater use of s. 8 powers.

(ii) that share or loan capital is not to be acquired unless the Secretary of State is satisfied that assistance cannot, or cannot appropriately, be given in any other way (s. 8 (3), amended). This repeal places s. 8 powers on a par with the amended powers of s. 7.

(iii) that the Secretary of State may not acquire more than half of the nominal value of the equity share capital of a company (s. 8 (3) (*b*), repealed). This amendment gives the Secretary of State the same freedom from limitation in respect of the percentage shareholding he may hold under s. 8 as he has always had under s. 7.

(iv) that the Secretary of State must dispose of shares or stock as soon as, in his opinion, it is reasonably practicable to do so (s. 8 (4), repealed); and

(v) that the powers under s. 8 expire at the end of 1977 (s. 8 (5), repealed).

The provision requiring the Secretary of State to seek an affirmative order from the House of Commons for a sum in excess of £5m in respect of any one project, is unaffected. [82]

There are no guidelines for the operation of the powers of s. 8. There is no specific criterion comparable to the employment criterion of s. 7. Certain issues are, of course, important in terms of the "national interest", notably possible effects on the balance of payments. [83]

The national interest is not defined, however, but the Treasury insist that there is a common understanding between the various departments concerned of what it constitutes including, in particular, close regard to the increased competitiveness of British industry (Expenditure Committee, Trade and Industry Sub-Committee, HC189–XXI, Minute of Evidence 24 June, 1975, Treasury Memorandum T60). [84]

However platitudinous this statement may be, there is a genuine difficulty in isolating any class of situation beyond those involving the reduction of employment, where State intervention is justifiable on the grounds of a disparity between public and private costs. Each situation is judged "on its merits". [85]

In the year ending 31st March 1975 there were 26 applications under s. 8, of which 8 were withdrawn and 10 offers of assistance made. Total expenditure under this section exceeds £127m. The amended provisions of s. 7 and s. 8 of the Industry Act 1972 are conveniently set out in Sch. 4, Part II, of the Industry Act 1975. [86]

DELEGATION OF THE SECRETARY OF STATE'S POWERS TO THE NATIONAL ENTERPRISE BOARD

The Secretary of State, may, with the consent of the Treasury and after consultation with the National Enterprise Board, direct the Board to exercise his powers under ss. 7 and 8 of the Industry Act 1972, and it shall be the duty of the Board to give effect to any direction (s. 3). The Board is not capable of exercising these powers unless specifically directed to do so by the Secretary of State, who therefore retains overall control and responsibility. It is envisaged that the N.E.B. will normally be used for the provision of finance under ss. 7

and 8 where large-scale assistance is required for major companies. The Government will normally have acquired equity and loan interests in the recipient companies in return for such assistance and it was felt by the Government that the deployment of the expertise which the N.E.B. will have at its disposal, in its holding company role, would be a better means of monitoring the performance of assisted companies than the present supervision, exercised directly by the Department of Industry. Furthermore, with such interests vested in the N.E.B. the Board could secure for itself—in so far as it is possible—the benefit of any increases in profitability which it may secure (though interests acquired under s. 3 will be separately accounted for, and separate financial determinations will be made in respect of such assets: see para. [**57**], *ante*). [**87**]

In passing, it should be noted that, corresponding with the delegation of ss. 7 and 8 powers to the Secretaries of State for Scotland and Wales, these powers can be devolved upon the Scottish and Welsh Development Agencies, respectively (Scottish Development Agency Act 1975, s. 5; Welsh Development Agency Act 1975, s. 12). [**88**]

The points which a direction under s. 3 may cover are set out in s. 3 (4), namely the purpose and manner in which the Board are to exercise the powers, the amount of assistance that it is to give and the terms and conditions on which the assistance is to be given. But the use of the word "may" in s. 3 (4) permits the Secretary of State some discretion over the degree of detail he wishes to include in the direction. As soon as is practicable after the Board has been directed, the Secretary of State must lay before each House of Parliament a statement specifying the amount of assistance, how and to whom it is to be given, and, if the aid is authorised by s. 7 powers, the assisted area in which the undertaking for which it is to be provided is or will be situated (s. 3 (6)). This is a departure from the provisions of the Industry Act 1972 which merely insisted that details of ss. 7 and 8 assistance should be included in an Annual Report, published no later than six months after the end of the financial year to which it relates (Industry Act 1972, s. 16 (1)). (Assistance under s. 8 which exceeded £5m could be the subject of a Parliamentary debate prior to an affirmative resolution, and this remains unchanged.) Furthermore, the Board's report for any accounting year will specify each direction under s. 3 and recount the information contained in the Parliamentary Statement (s. 3 (7)). The Annual Report of the Industry Act 1972 will also include a report of the delegation of ss. 7 and 8 powers (Sch. 7 (2)). Lastly, the Government has undertaken to publish details of assistance under ss. 7 and 8 at three-monthly intervals in the Department's journal "Trade and Industry". [**89**]

Laudable as these developments may be, it is clear that not all the details of Government assistance will be made public either in statements laid before Parliament or in the Annual Reports of the Act 1972 and the National Enterprise Board, or indeed, in "Trade and Industry". This is presumably because the information may be of a commercially sensitive nature and if published, may jeopardise private sector participation. The Government was berated in Committee for participating in ". . . a sordid traffic in secrecy" but the anodyne amendment represented by s. 3 (6) has done little to change the situation. The most potent way in which information can be elicited from Government remains the Parliamentary Question. [**90**]

When the Secretary of State gives aid under the provisions of the Industry Act 1972, it can be withdrawn or its terms varied, where appropriate. Likewise, if the N.E.B. acts under a direction the Secretary of State can revoke or amend the original direction by simply issuing a further direction. Indeed, the N.E.B. is under a duty to draw to the Department of Industry's attention any developments which might require a variation in the terms of a direction ("Guidelines", para. 24). But it is, and will remain, the Government's practice, when dispensing aid under s. 8 powers or when delegating such powers to the N.E.B., to conclude a contract with the company concerned and it is not intended that a new direction could be used to override a subsisting contract.   [**91**]

If the Government feel that payments, loans or whatever other form of assistance, had been applied in a way contrary to the contractual arrangement then its remedy will lie in an action for breach of contract.   [**92**]

A subsequent direction, therefore, will not relieve the Board of any contractual liability to which it is subject in consequence of an earlier direction (s. 3 (5)).   [**93**]

INDUSTRIAL DEVELOPMENT ADVISORY BOARD

As described earlier (para. (**11**), *ante*) the Secretary of State has the power to consult the I.D.A.B. before arriving at a decision regarding assistance to a company. Occasionally, as with the affairs of Court Line Ltd. (875 HC Deb. (1973–74), col. 1556) it was judged impossible in view of the urgency of the situation, to consult with the I.D.A.B. On other occasions, advice was sought and subsequently ignored by the Secretary of State. The Industry Act 1975 extends the I.D.A.B's responsibilities to the exercise of the Secretary of State's functions under s. 3 of the Act (Sch. 4, para. 5). Furthermore, the I.D.A.B. *must* be consulted on all applications which might subsequently be the subject of an s. 3 direction to the N.E.B. ("Guidelines", para. 36).   [**94**]

THE GOVERNMENT'S FINANCIAL LIABILITY TO THE BOARD

In general, the Secretary of State will compensate the N.E.B. for costs incurred in providing services to the Government or in undertaking functions at the Secretary of State's direction under s. 3.   [**95**]

Where the Board acquires property following a direction, the Secretary of State will reimburse the Board the consideration given for the acquisition and the costs and expenses of and incidental to it (s. 3 (9)). The word "property" has a wide meaning. The clear intention is to embrace all types of shares. Although the Secretary of State will reimburse the costs and expenses of acquiring the property these expenses will count towards the Board's capital debt, under Sch. 2, para. 6 (2) (*b*), but not towards the financial limit in s. 8 (2).   [**96**]

Equally, the Board will be reimbursed the cost of making any grants under s. 3, including interest relief grants and removal grants (s. 3 (10)). Where the Board makes a loan, following a direction, the Secretary of State will make a loan of the same amount and on corresponding terms, subject only to the Board's not being required to repay the loan to the Secretary of State until the debt has been repaid to the Board. In other words, if the ultimate borrower defaults the Board is relieved of any losses which it may have incurred in acting as the agent of the Secretary of State (s. 3 (11) (12)). In the event of the Board guaranteeing a loan from a third party to an ailing company, or giving insurance against default, the Secretary of State will relieve the Board of any losses sustained; it will assume a "correlative" liability (s. 3 (13)). Lastly, the Secretary of State has discretion to pay administrative expenses incurred by the Board, in administering ss. 7 and 8 assistance. This is a permissive power to enable the Secretary of State to reject unreasonable expenses and to cease payments in respect of particular companies which, having been restored to a satisfactory trading position, represent sound investments generating sufficient income to cover administrative expenses. [**97**]

GOVERNMENTAL LIABILITY TO THIRD PARTIES

Following the Government's power to reimburse moneys expended by the N.E.B. or to assume a "correlative" liability, there was strong pressure on the Government, during the bill's parliamentary passage, to extend the Government's "correlative" liability to creditors and shareholders of companies to which aid had been given. The Government felt no duty to assume the role of insurer of the risks of third parties trading with Government assisted companies. Nor did it introduce an Official Trustee who would take over temporary responsibility for companies in difficulty as proposed in the "Regeneration of British Industry", Cmnd. 5710 (1974), para. 34. [**98**]

In his commentary to the Annual Report of the Industry Act 1972 (HC 620 of 1974–75, p. 17) the Chairman of the Industrial Development Advisory Board referred to the fact that the greater part of the Board's deliberations ". . . concerned assistance to help companies in acute liquidity difficulties; these accounted for more than half the proposals that came before the Board . . . too many cases are brought to the Department of Industry only when the immediacy of the requirement for additional finance is such that no reasonable appraisal of the facts or the prospects of future viability can be properly considered by the Department or by the Board". In other words, prior to the decision regarding assistance, some of the companies seeking assistance were in a perilous situation, perhaps even insolvent. But for the prospect of Government assistance, creditors would have exercised their rights to attempt to obtain recovery of their debts and withdraw further credit facilities. [**99**]

Three questions are posed:

(i) Does the reasonable and honest expectation of Government assistance, or continued Government assistance, permit the company to continue to trade without the directors necessarily coming within the proscription of s. 332 (1) of the Companies Act 1948?

(ii) Is the Government, with knowledge of the company's reasonable expectation, or reliance upon aid already given, a party to the company continuing to trade while insolvent and therefore possibly liable within the terms of s. 332 (1)?

(iii) Is there any general principle of public policy requiring the Government to indemnify creditors of companies which have been formed by the

Government, or heavily subsidised by the Government, or which have been used as an agent or instrument of Government policy?

The answers to these questions must remain speculative but may be of interest to the trader contracting with a company seeking or in receipt of assistance, or to a prospective or actual creditor of such a company.   [**100**]

The Companies Act 1948, s. 332 (1), reads thus:

> "If the course of the winding up of a company it appears that any business of the company has been carried on with intent to defraud creditors of the company or creditors of any other person or for any fraudulent purpose, the court, on the application of the official receiver, or the liquidator or any creditor or contributory of the company, may, if it thinks proper so to do, declare that any persons who were knowingly parties to the carrying on of the business in manner aforesaid shall be personally responsible, without any limitation of liability, for all or any of the debts or other liabilities of the company as the court may direct."

The important question flowing from the above is discovering whether or not the business of the company was carried on with intent to defraud creditors of the company. It is for the liquidator, receiver or creditor to discharge the heavy burden of proving fraud. But the existence of intent may be inferred from the way in which the business is carried on.   [**101**]

"If a company continues to carry on business and to incur debts at a time when there is, to the knowledge of the directors, no reasonable prospect of the creditors ever receiving payment of those debts, it is, in general, a proper inference that the company is carrying on business with intent to defraud." *Re William C. Leitch Bros., Ltd.*, [1932] 2 Ch. 71, 77, *per* Maugham, J.   [**102**]

In a later case, Maugham, J., returned to s. 275 of the Companies Act 1929 (almost equivalent to s. 332 of the 1948 Act; under the 1929 Act the power to make declarations was limited to directors only). Stating that he was not attempting a definition of fraud, but rather of one of the elements of the word as used in this section, he remarked, ". . . the words 'defraud' and 'fraudulent purpose', where they appear in the section in question, are words which connote actual dishonesty involving, according to current notions of fair trading among commercial men, real moral blame". *Re Patrick and Lyon, Ltd.*, [1933] Ch. 786, at pp. 790–791.   [**103**]

Thus, it is to the judgement of ordinary commercial men to which one must turn to ascertain whether the expectation, on the part of directors, of Government assistance is reasonable, and whether such assistance would be sufficient to allow creditors a reasonable prospect of receiving payment of debts incurred.   [**104**]

From the Government's viewpoint, it is clear that though the Crown is not bound by the provisions of s. 332 of the Companies Act 1948 Government representatives have repeatedly stated that they will honour any obligation which in the absence of privilege, may arise (Third Report from the Committee of Public Accounts, HC 447 of 1971–72, Q.1599, Evidence of Sir Anthony Part).   [**105**]

The Government's view of its obligations is expressed in a written answer by the then Chief Secretary to the Treasury: ". . . I am concerned that there should be no misunderstanding as to the position of creditors in relation to limited liability companies in which the Government has a financial interest— for example, as creditor, minority or sole shareholder. I should make it absolutely plain that those doing business with such a company must act on the assumption that liability for the company's debts will be determined solely in accordance with the normal rules applicable to a limited liability company under the Companies Acts except where the Government undertake or have undertaken a specific commitment in relation to those debts" (832 HC WA (1970–71), col. 282). The statement does not deny that the Government may be responsible for a company's debts, only that it will not *necessarily* assume such responsibility. This position is substantially repeated in the N.E.B. "Guidelines", where it is stated (at para. 12) ". . . the practice of the N.E.B. in relation to companies in which it has a minority shareholding will have regard to the practice of companies in the private sector in relation to their subsidiaries. There will be no Government guarantee to the creditors of (such) companies unless the Government has undertaken a specific commitment in relation to a company's debts."

[**106**]

In other words, the Government is seeking to rid itself of the appearance of estoppel based upon its superior knowledge of the company's affairs. (This is doubly true if not all details of Governmental assistance are made public.) It is a matter of evidence in each case whether the Government or N.E.B. is "knowingly" a party to the business being carried on while insolvent. The contrary is an unlikely card for Government to play, though it did seek at one point to limit the information it received from Upper Clyde Shipbuilders Ltd. during that company's progression toward liquidation, in order to reduce the danger of s. 332 liability (Third Report, Q.3128, Evidence of Mr. E. V. Marchant). [**107**]

A difficulty arises, however, in deciding whether the Government, though privy to a company trading while insolvent, is actually a "party" to such trading within the meaning of s. 332 (1). In the course of his judgment in *Re Maidstone Buildings Provisions, Ltd.*, [1971] 3 All E.R. 363, at p. 368, Pennycuick, V.C., stated that a party ". . . participates in . . . takes part in . . . concurs in . . ." the running of the business. A mere financier, therefore, of an insolvent company would not, of necessity, be liable under s. 332; nor, following the learned judge, would an omission or failure to discharge a duty lead to personal liability. But in the situations in which Governments have been involved, there has usually been a substantial State shareholding, Government nominees as directors and direct involvement on the part of the State in important financial decisions affecting the company. The Government has therefore become not merely privy, but party, to the running of the company. [**108**]

It is submitted, also, that governmental liability is not contingent on the liability of the directors. This is because Government or the N.E.B. possesses or ought to possess knowledge regarding future financial assistance to the company which may not be available to the board. Notwithstanding the Chief Secretary's statement that the Government will not automatically be liable, provided the conditions are satisfied the Secretary of State or N.E.B. nominees may be personally liable for all the debts of the Government assisted or formerly

Government assisted company. But this must remain a tentative conclusion.
[**109**]

Finally, there may be situations, such as that which obtained in the matter
of Beagle Aircraft, Ltd., where irrespective of liability under s. 332 and notwithstanding the absence of any "intent to defraud" the Government indemni-
fied all creditors (796 HC Deb., col. 177). It is difficult to generalise from such a
situation; Beagle was wholly owned by the Government, every director was a
Government nominee and the Government had not stated its position in
relation to the company's debts. But it is at least suggestive that the creditors
of companies which are intimately connected with Government policy, perhaps
formed at the insistence of Government and having to fulfil a mixture of social
and economic obligations may receive an indemnity in the event of withdrawal
of Government financial assistance. It is almost invariably the case that such a
company would have been liquidated but for the promise and reality of
Government support. [**110**]

It is perhaps appropriate that if a company is used as a vehicle for public
policy its cost should be borne by public funds rather than by private
creditors. (It is understood that a similar case was argued by the Official
Liquidator of Upper Clyde Shipbuilders Ltd. to the Department of Industry,
but to no avail.) [**111**]

THE OMBUDSMAN

The use of the Industry Act 1972 powers by the Secretary of State and the
Department of Industry come within the sphere of responsibility of the Parliamentary Commissioner for Administration and his competence to inquire into
maladministration under the Parliamentary Commissioner Act 1967. If these
powers are delegated and exercised by the N.E.B. the Ombudsman has no
authority over the activities of the Board. [**112**]

The Government resisted an attempt to amend Sch. 2 of the Parliamentary
Commissioner Act 1967 to include the N.E.B.: it was thought inappropriate
that the jurisdiction of the Ombudsman, who is concerned to ensure proper
standards of public administration, should apply to the body whose standards
are likely to be commercial. The decision specifically to direct the N.E.B. to
assume the powers vested in the Secretary of State is under the surveillance of
the Ombudsman, who may seek documents and evidence from the Board. This
decision is clearly in the domain of public administration; but the subsequent
activities of the N.E.B. represent its exercise of commercial judgement and,
in common with maladministration in nationalised industries, is not under the
scrutiny of the Ombudsman. In any event, the Ombudsman is precluded from
examining the Government's contractual or commercial activities by virtue of
Sch. 3 of the 1967 Act. Furthermore, the Ombudsman has power not to proceed
with a matter if a right in law exists, and it would be reasonable for the com-
plainant to seek legal redress (e.g. the situation facing a creditor of a company
which has gone into liquidation following the withdrawal of Government
financial assistance). [**113**]

The Industry Act 1975 makes a number of additional amendments to the
Industry Act 1972 and to the Development of Inventions Act 1967 which are

perhaps best dealt with in the context of selective financial assistance to industry. [**114**]

SHIPBUILDING

The Industry Act 1972, s. 10, is amended so as to increase the limits on the liabilities which the Secretary of State may assume in the giving of guarantees under the section. The liabilities which the Secretary of State may assume were previously limited by s. 10 (3) to £1,000m, a figure which had been increased by Statutory Instrument to a maximum of £1,400m (Ships and Mobile Offshore Installations Construction Credits (Increase of Limit) Order 1975, S.I. 1975 No. 138). The amendment increases the limit to £1,800m (s. 23).

The purpose of the Home Credit Scheme is to give U.K. shipowners, ordering at home, access to credit facilities comparable to those available abroad. In the absence of such a scheme, there would be a financial incentive for a U.K. owner to place his order abroad. [**115**]

The Home Credit Scheme was introduced by the Shipbuilding Industry Act 1967 with a limit of £200m. This limit was successively increased, by the Shipbuilding Industry Acts 1969 and 1971, to £400m and to £700m. [**116**]

Under the Shipbuilding Industry Acts a guarantee could not be given without a recommendation from the Shipbuilding Industry Board that certain criteria were satisfied concerning the reorganisation of the shipbuilder's resources. The administration of the scheme was in this way linked with the implementation of the recommendations of the Geddes Committee. With the completion of the Geddes programme and the demise of the Shipbuilding Industry Board at the end of 1971 power was taken under this section to continue the scheme without reference to the reorganisation of resources; to extend its application to include mobile off-shore installations; and to increase the limit to £1,000m with power further to increase it to £1,400m by Order. [**117**]

Section 10 also provides for the refinancing of credit on the lines described in a statement by the Minister for Trade on 15th March 1972. This covered new arrangements for the financing of fixed rate export credit as well as home shipbuilding credit. [**118**]

Sub-section (1)

Under this sub-section the Secretary of State may guarantee the repayment of sums advanced to individuals resident and companies incorporated in the United Kingdom (including the Channel Islands and the Isle of Man) to finance orders placed by them for the construction of ships and mobile off-shore installations in the United Kingdom. In practice, guarantees are given on loans made by the clearing banks. [**119**]

The Act does not specify the terms on which guaranteed credit is made available to borrowers. In practice, we follow the O.E.C.D. Export Credit Understanding for Ships to which the U.K. and all major shipbuilding nations subscribe. This currently provides that credit shall not exceed 70% of the contract price of a ship; that the maximum period of the loan is 7 years from delivery; and that the minimum interest rate should be 8%. The U.K. with a number of other O.E.C.D. nations observes the minimum interest rate on the basis of $7\frac{1}{2}$% plus charges, bringing the effective cost of credit up to the level stipulated in the Understanding. There is provision in the O.E.C.D. Understanding for variation of the terms when necessary to match credits offered by non-signatory countries. [**120**]

Qualifying size—Guarantees may only be given in respect of ships and mobile installations of the qualifying size. This is defined in s. 12 (2) of the Act as meaning in the case of ships 100 gross tons and in the case of mobile off-shore installations 100 tons, excluding fuel and water. [**121**]

Mobile off-shore installations—The sub-section makes specific mention of mobile off-shore installations (as defined in s. 12 (1)) in order that the eligibility of these structures for credit guarantees under the Home Credit Scheme should be put beyond question. [**122**]

No express provision for mobile off-shore installations was made in the Shipbuilding Industry Acts 1967, 1969 and 1971 and credit guarantees under those Acts could be given only for constructions of "ships". Up to the introduction of the 1972 Act therefore, only off-shore structures that could be legally regarded as "ships" had been eligible for the Home Credit Scheme. The definition in s. 12 (1), however, covers all kinds of installations used for underwater exploration or exploitation of mineral resources which are intended to move from place to place without major dismantling or modification. [**123**]

The definition does not cover fixed installations which once they have been established on a particular site cannot be moved without being dismantled. Such installations are used in the *production* of oil and natural gas (as distinct from mobile installations used for explorations) and are usually built by civil engineers, though some of the work may be sub-contracted to shipbuilders. Credit facilities for the construction of fixed installations is a separate issue outside the field of shipbuilding policy. [**124**]

Administration—The Ship Mortgage Finance Company advises the Department, as it has done from the outset of the scheme, on security for guaranteed loans and acts as the Department's agent in negotiations with shipowners. There have been no cases of default under the scheme. [**125**]

Sub-section (2)

This sub-section places a limit on the total liability the Secretary of State may incur under guarantees given by him under the Home Credit Scheme. The provision follows in form the precedent of the Shipbuilding Industry Acts 1967 and 1971 and follows the earlier Acts in providing that if there is a default and the Secretary of State is obliged to honour a guarantee, any amounts paid out and not recovered must be deducted from the limit. [**126**]

Sub-section (3)

This sub-section provides that the amounts guaranteed shall not exceed £1,000 million, but this may, with the consent of the Treasury, be raised by order to a maximum of £1,400 million. [**127**]

Sub-section (4)

This sub-section provides that the power by order to raise the limit to £1,400 million shall be subject to the approval of the House of Commons. [**128**]

Sub-section (5)

This sub-section gives the Secretary of State power to make loans to any person who has provided finance under the Scheme. The power was required to give effect to the new arrangements for refinancing credits for shops and exports which were announced in Parliament by the Minister for Trade on 15th March 1972 HC Deb 833 col. 535-41. [**129**]

Up to that time the banks had provided home shipbuilding finance (and long-term finance for exports) from their own resources at a fixed rate of interest agreed between them and the Government. By 1969 the sums involved (particularly for exports) had become very large and the banks were given refinancing rights with the Issue Department of the Bank of England to the extent that the volume of their lending exceeded 10% of their total deposits. By 1972 this arrangement was becoming unsatisfactory in two ways. The fixed rate of interest provided the banks with a relatively low return during a period of high interest rates; and the amount of refinancing undertaken by the Issue Department began to hamper the Issue Department's market management functions. [**130**]

New arrangements were therefore worked out between the Government and the banks. It was agreed that the banks would continue to provide all the initial finance, thus preserving the relationship between them and their customers. To the extent that their total lending (for exports and home ship-building) exceeds 18% of their current account deposits they would be refinanced by the Government (instead of the the Issue Department). The return to the banks on that part of their lending which they financed themselves would no longer necessarily be the same as the fixed rate paid by the shipowner (or exporter). It would instead vary broadly in line with market rates in accordance with an agreed formula recalculated each month. That formula was the average of the Treasury Bill yield and the Clearing Banks' syndicated lending rate for nationalised industries, plus a margin of $1\frac{1}{4}\%$ to allow, in particular, for the fact that the banks are tying up their funds for a period of years in unmarketable assets. The fixed rate of lending to shipowners was to be determined by the Government alone and in accordance with Britain's O.E.C.D. obligations. Any difference between the agreed rate of return to the banks and the fixed rate at which credit is advanced by them was to be settled through an adjustment in the interest payable by the banks on the amounts refinanced by the Government. [**131**]

Those arrangements came into effect on 16th March 1972. Refinance for exports was provided by the E.C.G.D. under the Export Guarantee Act 1968. Refinance for shipbuilding continued to be provided by the Issue Department until the Industry Act became law in August 1972. The Issue Department loans are gradually being taken over by the Secretary of State. [**132**]

Sub-section (6)

This sub-section provides that the aggregate amount of refinancing loans shall not exceed the aggregate amount of the Secretary of State's liability under guarantees given by him under this section and s. 7 of the Shipbuilding Industry Act 1967. As explained in the note on sub-section (5), only a proportion of the loans guaranteed under the Home Credit Scheme are in fact refinanced. However, no precise estimate could be made in advance of what this proportion would be. It was necessary therefore to adopt as the limit the total outstanding liability under guarantees, though in practice the amount of the loans falls well short of this limit.   [**133**]

Sub-section (7)

This sub-section enables the Secretary of State to provide guarantees and loans on such terms and conditions as may be agreed with the approval of the Treasury.   [**134**]

Refinance lending—Agreements have been entered into by the Secretary of State with each of the banks involved in the scheme. These agreements stipulate the terms and conditions under which the refinancing arrangements are to operate.   [**135**]

Guarantees—In considering applications for guaranteed credit the Department applies rules intended to limit the amount of foreign content in a ship for which a guarantee is given. These rules follow E.C.G.D. practice and the requirements of E.E.C.   [**136**]

Sub-section (8)

This sub-section follows the precedent of the Shipbuilding Industry Act 1967. It provides that in calculating, for the purpose of the limits prescribed in the Section, the aggregate of the Secretary of State's liabilities no account is to be taken of interest. Liability in respect of interest was excluded because it would not be practicable to calculate it with any precision.   [**137**]

Sub-section (9)

The wording of this sub-section follows that in the Shipbuilding Industry Act 1967. Construction is defined as including the completion of a partially completed ship or installation and a guarantee can thus be given in respect of a loan to a U.K. owner to finance the completion of a partially constructed ship or installation in a U.K. yard.   [**138**]

Such cases seldom arise but may occur, e.g., on the collapse of the original builder when the ship or installation is completed by another builder.   [**139**]

The Industry Act 1972, s. 10, is further amended by s. 24 of the Industry Act 1975, thus enabling the Secretary of State to transfer from one company to another in the same group the benefit of a guarantee given under the Home Credit Scheme for shipbuilding.   [**140**]

The power to transfer guarantees is not required for use in general since the objective of the Home Credit Scheme is to secure orders for U.K. shipyards and there is no particular reason why a different shipowner, who did not place the original order, should get the benefit of the guarantee and the fixed interest loan that goes with it. The original working of s. 10 (1) of the Industry Act 1972, however, prevented the transference of a guarantee even when the liability to repay a loan passes from one company to another in the same group. In such a case there was in general no change in the ultimate liability to repay the loan, since the liability remained within the same group of companies. Accordingly, there was no reason to refuse a transfer. The fact that the Secretary of State could not have agreed to it has apparently proved inconvenient when shipping groups wished to reorganise, for example, by putting all their ships and the associated loans within a single company. [141]

The reorganisation must be undertaken for genuine purposes only. Clearly, the benefit of a guarantee could be transferred under this section, to a company outside the group by the device of forming a new subsidiary company, transferring the guaranteed loan to it, and then selling the shares in the company to outside interests. The Secretary of State can, however, prevent this since it is normally made a condition of a guarantee that his consent is required to the sale of shares in subsidiary companies which have received loans under the Home Credit Scheme. [142]

Two new sub-sections in s. 10 are authorised by s. 24 (1) Industry Act 1975:

Sub-section (7A) provides power to renew a guarantee (including a guarantee previously renewed) on the transfer of a liability from one company to another in the same group. The renewal requires Treasury consent, in parallel with the provision in s. 10 of the 1972 Act which requires Treasury consent to the original guarantee.

The sub-section refers not only to a liability but also to part of a liability. This is to cover cases in which the liability to repay a loan does not rest with a single company but is shared with others—for example, when the ownership of a ship is divided between two or more parties.

Sub-section (7B) explains that two companies are to be regarded as being in the same group if one is the other's holding company or both are subsidiaries of a third company. [143]

GRANTS TO SUPPLEMENT INTEREST

The last amendment to s. 10 of the 1972 Act enables the Secretary of State to make grants for the purpose of supplementing the interest received by the lenders (normally, the clearing banks) on loans to U.K. shipowners, under the Home Credit Scheme, to finance the construction of ships or mobile off-shore installations in U.K. shipyards (s. 25). The amendment was required because of difficulties in operating the fixed rate credit scheme for shipbuilding and exports. As part of the scheme introduced in March 1972 the clearing banks agreed to provide finance for shipbuilding and exports at fixed rates of interest determined by the Government. The rates were set for shipbuilding to accord with the O.E.C.D. Understanding on export credits for ships and for exports, within a range, in the light of the rates available from our major overseas competitors. In return the banks received from the Department of Industry (for shipbuilding) and from the E.C.G.D. (for exports) firstly, refinancing loans in respect of that part of each clearing bank's total fixed rate lending which was in excess of 18% of its current account balances averaged over the previous twelve months, and secondly, an agreed rate of return on the unrefinanced shipbuilding and export lending made at fixed rates. [144]

It was originally envisaged that the "interest supplement" due to the banks in respect of the difference between the fixed rate and the agreed rate would be paid to the bank by setting off the interest due from the banks to the Government on the refinancing loans. This arrangement worked well enough until commercial interest rates dramatically increased causing the gap between the fixed rate and the agreed rate to widen. In addition, the banks' current account balances increased so that the 18% threshold was higher than expected and thus smaller amounts were eligible for refinancing loans on which the Departments could earn interest. Correspondingly greater amounts were financed by the banks from their own resources. So, the interest supplement payable to the banks far exceeded the amount of interest due from them on the refinancing loans. [145]

No power to pay interest to the banks was included in the 1972 Act, and the E.C.G.D. had no such power. Because of this deficiency in powers the arrears of "interest supplement" had risen by October 1974 to £25.5m in respect of shipbuilding and £85.9m in respect of exports. Following a review of the situation a revised scheme was implemented with effect from 17th October 1974 and the arrears of interest were paid on 15th January 1975. The payment was made under the authority of the Consolidated Fund (No. 4) Act 1974. The scheme has the same framework as the previous one, with the important difference that by providing for adjustments to be made to the level of the agreed rate of return which the banks receive on unrefinanced lending, it is expected to produce savings in public expenditure. (Similar powers to those conferred on the Secretary of State are given to the E.C.G.D.; see the Export Guarantees Act 1975, s. 3 (1) (*b*).) [146]

Further amendments to the Industry Act 1972 are outlined in Sch. 7, which takes effect by virtue of s. 39 (2). Paragraph 1 removes the reference to a "pipe-line" in the definition of "machinery or plant" and "works" in s. 6 (2) of the 1972 Act. As a consequence of this deletion the word "pipe-line" no longer appears in the Act and Sch. 8 consequently also deletes the definition of "pipe-line". The 1972 Act as drafted specifically excluded pipe-lines from eligibility for Regional Development Grants: they are now eligible for such a grant. The purpose of this amendment is to simplify the administration of Regional Development Grants by making it unnecessary to decide whether any particular pipe or associated apparatus is a pipe-line within the meaning of the Pipe-lines Act 1962 and therefore ineligible for grant. In fact, the Government has regarded as eligible all pipe-lines on qualifying premises except those which do not form part of the equipment of the premises since at least November 1973. The amendment merely legitimates the current practice. [147]

AMENDMENT OF DEVELOPMENT OF INVENTIONS ACT 1967

Although the Industry Act 1975 is hardly the appropriate vehicle to effect changes to the Development of Inventions Act 1967, it was felt that the following provision should be inserted (s. 26). [148]

The Development of Inventions Act 1967, s. 4, is amended to raise the limit above which the National Research Development Corporation (N.R.D.C.) must obtain Ministerial approval, from £1,000 to £20,000 in individual cases. The original limit was established in 1954 and has not been increased since. In future, the Secretary of State may revise the limit by means of a Statutory Instrument, subject to the negative resolution procedure. [149]

Section 4 of the 1967 Act specifies the activities of the N.R.D.C. requiring Ministerial approval. In summary, they are:

(1) the carrying out by or on behalf of the N.R.D.C. of any project for the making of goods, the construction of works or the provision of services (except for anything done only by way of experiment or trial);

(2) the provision of financial assistance to any person or body developing or exploiting an invention (except where the amount of assistance does not exceed £1,000, now £20,000);

(3) the acquisition of any undertaking or taking shares in a body corporate carrying on an understanding;

(4) the promotion or assistance of research.   [**150**]

CHAPTER 4

TRANSFERS OF CONTROL OF IMPORTANT MANUFACTURING UNDERTAKINGS TO NON-RESIDENTS

The provisions of Part II of the Industry Act 1975 give statutory effect to the statement in para. 33 of the White Paper entitled "The Regeneration of British Industry" (Cmnd. 5710): "If in any case compulsory acquisition proved to be necessary this would normally be authorised by a specific Act of Parliament. *If unforeseeable developments of compelling urgency were to arise—for example the imminent failure or loss to foreign control of an important company in a key sector of manufacturing industry—the Government would bring the issue before Parliament, and any action would require specific parliamentary approval.*"

[**151**]

Powers to make orders dealing with the prohibition of certain acts ("prohibition orders") and with the compulsory acquisition of shares or of assets ("vesting orders") are conferred on the Secretary of State by s. 13 and apply when a "change of a control" of an "important manufacturing undertaking" has occurred or is about to occur. Subsequent sections define the parliamentary arrangements for these orders, contain provisions about the contents of vesting orders, limit the territorial scope of prohibition orders and make provision for the making of "compensation orders" prior to the transfer of capital or assets to the Government or N.E.B. [**152**]

These powers are confined to situations where there is a "serious and immediate probability" of an important United Kingdom manufacturing company falling into foreign hands and where, in the opinion of the Secretary of State, this would be contrary to the interests of the United Kingdom; or to situations where such a transfer has come to the notice of the Secretary of State within a limited period. It is noteworthy that the provisions to be described contain the only reference in the Act to the compulsory acquisition of undertakings and though the Secretary of State is endowed with discretionary powers, which permit little possibility of judicial review, elaborate provisions have been inserted ensuring parliamentary scrutiny and control of the exercise of such powers. These powers are more extensive than those found in s. 2 (2) (c) (extending public ownership into profitable areas of manufacturing industry). In addition to the explicit compulsion found in s. 13 powers, the Secretary of State has the power to nationalise certain elements of an undertaking (see para. [154], *post*). But there is no comparable provision in s. 2 (2) (c) for the acquisition of only part of the assets of a company; here, the company is acquired following a market or voluntary sale. There is no necessity for the valuation of the company to be referred to arbitration. If it is remembered that many major enterprises are heavily diversified, the prospect of acquiring assets *via* s. 2 (2) (c), which may have little relevance to whatever strategy is being pursued by the purchase, is one that is unlikely to appeal to the N.E.B.

[153]

MEANING OF IMPORTANT MANUFACTURING UNDERTAKING

The Secretary of State's power to make orders prohibiting certain actions or acquiring shares or assets is limited to the situation where an important manufacturing undertaking faces or suffers a change of control (s. 11 (1)). An "important manufacturing undertaking" is defined as: ". . . an undertaking which, in so far as it is carried on in the United Kingdom, is wholly or mainly engaged in manufacturing industry and appears to the Secretary of State to be of special importance to the United Kingdom or to any substantial part of the United Kingdom" (s. 11 (2)). "Undertaking" means simply "business concern", and its use ensures broader coverage than would result from defining the powers in relation to the business or assets of a company only. "Undertaking" could embrace administrative units such as divisions of companies and cover businesses which have not been incorporated, and possibly, even the business of a holding company and its subsidiaries where that could reasonably be viewed as a single undertaking. [154]

It is not necessary that the operations in the United Kingdom should form the whole, or even the major part, of the undertaking in question, but its United Kingdom activities must be wholly or mainly in manufacturing. Manufacturing industry is broadly defined as Standard Industrial Classification Orders III–XIX, together with the activities noted in s. 37 (3). [155]

No definition is offered of ". . . special importance to the United Kingdom or to any substantial part . . ." This is presumably because there are many ways in which an undertaking can assume importance, for instance, by virtue of its contribution to exports, employment, technological developments, defence contracts and so forth. The undertaking's contribution can also be to "a substantial part" of the United Kingdom. "A substantial part", the delineation of which is left to the Secretary of State, denotes a region or at the very least a substantial part of a region. This ensures that a company of great importance to a particular region can claim the protection of the provisions of Part II of the Act. The area contemplated is presumably greater than that envisaged in the Industry Act 1972, s. 8 (1) (a), which refers to ". . . any part or area of the United Kingdom", for the purposes of granting selective financial assistance.

[156]

MEANING OF CHANGE OF CONTROL

As originally presented to Parliament the Bill lacked any clearly defined notion of "control" and "change of control". It is likely that the Secretary of State would have had regard to the wide definition of the Fair Trading Act 1973, s. 65, which provides that control is exercised when "a person or group of persons . . . are able directly or indirectly, to control or materially to influence the policy of a body corporate . . . without having a controlling interest in that body . . .". The Government yielded to pressure and the Act adopts a numerical or objective notion of control.   **[157]**

Reflecting the principles of City Code on Takeovers and Mergers, "control" is defined as where an individual or body corporate is entitled to cast 30% or more of the votes that may be cast at any general meeting or has the power to direct the holder of shares or stock as to the exercise of his votes at a general meeting. Similarly, if an individual or body corporate controls one body corporate which in turn has control of another body corporate, control of the latter body is vested in the individual or body corporate (s. 12 (3) (a)).   **[158]**

A change of control *only* occurs once one of five "relevant events" has happened. (It should be noted that when a change of control of a business comes about through changes in the control of a company which carries it on, it occurs only when one of the qualifying percentages is reached: change of control is defined in numerical terms and *cannot* take place in any other way.) A "relevant event" means any event as a result of which:

(i) the person carrying on the whole or part of the undertaking ceases to be resident in the United Kingdom;

(ii) a person not resident in the United Kingdom acquires the whole or part of the undertaking;

(iii) a body corporate resident in the United Kingdom but controlled by a person not so resident acquires the whole or part of the undertaking;

(iv) a person not resident in the United Kingdom becomes able to exercise or control the exercise of the first, second or third qualifying percentage of votes in a body corporate carrying on the whole or part of the undertaking or in any other body corporate which is in control of such a body; or

(v) a person resident in the United Kingdom and able to exercise or control the exercise of the first, second or third qualifying percentage of votes in a body corporate carrying the whole or part of the undertaking or in any other body corporate which is in control of such a body ceases to be resident in the United Kingdom (s. 12 (2)).   **[159]**

The circumstance outlined above in (i) describes the situation where the same person, natural or corporate, remains in control of a company but moves from the United Kingdom to become a resident abroad. This constitutes, within the terms of the Act, a "change of control". More obviously, (ii) refers to the situation where a non-resident acquires the whole or part of an undertaking. The wording would seem to cover the case in which control, already vested in a non-resident, is transferred to another non-resident. The third "relevant event" constituting a "change of control" is where a body corporate resident in the United Kingdom, and controlled by a person not so resident, acquires the whole or part of an undertaking. A body corporate will not be considered "resident" in the United Kingdom if it is not incorporated in the United Kingdom (s. 18 (2)). The last two "relevant events" refer to the situation where a non-resident is in a position to control the exercise of the first, second or third qualifying percentages in a body corporate carrying on the undertaking or in any other body corporate which is in control of such a body. The Act defines qualifying percentages as 30%, 40% and 50% of the votes that may be cast at a general meeting respectively (s. 12 (6)). The concept of qualifying percentages was introduced to counteract certain disadvantages flowing from defining "control" in numerical terms. The Government accepted that ownership of 30% of a company's shares need not necessarily give control in practice; control thereby acquired might be purely formal. In such cases the Government would not wish to invoke the powers found in Part II of the Act, yet failure to do so within three months would, in the absence of further qualification, prevent the Secretary of State proceeding further (s. 15 (4)). Without a time limit, under-takings which could become subject to a vesting order would never cease to be threatened and this would doubtless have an inhibiting effect on their manage-ment. Alternatively, with no notion of qualifying percentages, undertakings would be subject to vesting even though a "change of control", in practical terms, had not occurred. The qualifying percentages of 30%, 40% and 50% are designed to allow the Secretary of State the opportunity to act when any of the three levels have been attained, yet at the same time indicating to the purchaser that once a period of three months has elasped, no Government action will be taken, unless and until a further qualifying percentage has been reached.

[160]

A final provision relates to the situation where an acquisition is made by two or more persons acting in concert: this might, for example, occur when the acquisition was made through a number of nominees acting on behalf of a single principal. Such concerted action may be treated as the action of one person, for the purposes of Part II of the Act relating to change of control (s. 12 (5)). [161]

PROHIBITION ORDERS

The Secretary of State has the power to make orders to prevent the change of control of important manufacturing undertakings by means of a prohibition order. The conditions which, in the Secretary of State's opinion, must be satisfied before a prohibition order is made are set out in s. 13 (1):

(a) there must be a serious and immediate probability that there will be a change of control in an important manufacturing undertaking, as defined in s. 11 (2); and

(b) the change of control must be contrary to the interests of the United Kingdom or of any substantial part thereof.

There is no reason to believe that the national interest is defined solely in economic terms. The Secretary of State may take account, for instance, of defence interests and national prestige as well as employment, export and other considerations. In particular, the nationality of the purchaser is likely to be important. [162]

The prohibition order must specify the undertaking, prohibit the change of control and "prohibit or restrict the doing of things which (in the Secretary of

State's opinion) would constitute or lead to it; and may make such incidental or supplementary provision in the order as appears to him to be necessary or expedient" (s. 13 (1)). The power to prohibit actions constituting or leading to a change of control contrary to the national interest is comparable to the powers found in the Fair Trading Act 1973, s. 74 (1) (a), in relation to mergers which have been referred to the Monopolies Commission for consideration as to whether the conditions specified in that Act apply and if so, whether they would operate against the public interest. In fact, the wording of s. 13 (1) is somewhat broader in scope, ensuring that actions which would provide the basis for, but would not actually consummate, a change of control may be prohibited. The Act prevents, therefore, further acquisitions of shares even before the purchaser has reached the point of gaining control. [**163**]

The Act does not specify how a prohibition order should be effected, and there is sufficient latitude in the wording of the section for the Government to do almost anything. The action taken will very largely depend upon the circumstances surrounding the proposed change of control and if the proposed purchase has been carried out within the United Kingdom jurisdiction or not. "The drafting is deliberately rather loose to ensure that all such acts which are intended should be caught are caught." (For comparable vagueness see Fair Trading Act 1973, Sch. 8, para. 12.) It is clear, however, that the prohibition order will be personal to a particular purchaser or one group of purchasers and will not place a general prohibition on the share owners selling to any other potential purchasers who express an interest. [**164**]

TERRITORIAL SCOPE OF PROHIBITION ORDERS

A prohibition order cannot affect someone's actions and activities outside the United Kingdom, except where the person is:

(a) a citizen of the United Kingdom and Colonies, or
(b) a body corporate incorporated in the United Kingdom, or
(c) a person carrying on business in the United Kingdom either alone or in partnership (s. 18 (1)).

A prohibition order can therefore be extended to acts or omissions of individuals and companies included in the same categories wherever they may be. In fact, s. 18 (1) (c) refers to a "person" (not necessarily a citizen or a company incorporated in the United Kingdom), which extends the jurisdiction still further to the activities abroad of foreigners carrying on business in the United Kingdom. (A similar provision to s. 18 (1) is found in the Fair Trading Act 1973, s. 90 (3).) It will however be difficult for a prohibition order to cover the sale of a British undertaking from one foreign person to another, if both remain outside the United Kingdom, unless and until it is necessary to do something in the United Kingdom to effect completion. [**165**]

PARLIAMENTARY CONTROL OF PROHIBITION ORDERS

The making of a prohibition order does not require Parliamentary approval and comes into force as soon as it is made. It will lapse, however, if an affirmative resolution has not been passed in each House of Parliament, within twenty-eight days of the order being made. (The time limit does not include periods during which Parliament has been dissolved, prorogued or during which both Houses are adjourned for more than four days (s. 15 (1) (2).) Within the twenty-eight days a new order can be laid before Parliament thus giving the Government a measure of discretion should pressure on Parliamentary time prevent the seeking of approval from each House. If a prohibition order is not approved and so ceases to have effect after twenty-eight days, anything done under it during the twenty-eight days is nevertheless not affected. (Similar provisions are found in the Fair Trading Act 1973, s. 74, where only a negative resolution is required for approval.) [**166**]

The Industry Bill in its original form provided that no petition could be presented to Parliament either in respect of prohibition or vesting orders. After Parliamentary pressure was brought to bear on the Government, a "full" hybrid procedure is now available to those who doubt the suitability of a prohibition order and who have a legitimate interest to protect. [**167**]

A Bill is hybrid when it "affects a particular interest in a manner different from the private interest of other persons or bodies of the same category or class", and in these circumstances a Public Bill is subject to Private Bill procedure. Any Public Bill deemed hybrid in this way by the Commons Standing Orders Committee is submitted to a select committee which has power to receive petitions on the Bill. The Bill is subsequently recommitted to a standing committee or committee of the whole House and proceeds through report and subsequent stages as a Public Bill would normally. The petitioning stage is repeated in the Lords. In the Commons there is no special procedure applicable to subordinate legislation affecting private interests in a way which would, if included in a Bill, make the Bill hybrid. Subordinate legislation considered by the Lords, however—orders requiring an affirmative resolution—may also be deemed hybrid under Standing Order 216 of the Lords, under which the order is referred to the Lords Special Orders Committee, after which anyone with *locus standi* may petition within fourteen days. There is normally a minimum period of thirty-two days between an order deemed hybrid being laid and its coming into effect. It was the delay caused by the near-inevitability of a petition that prompted the Government originally not to permit such a procedure. In the Act, however, a full hybrid procedure has been adopted in the case of prohibition orders: such orders are immediately applicable and can be renewed. [**168**]

REMEDIES FOR CONTRAVENTION OF PROHIBITION ORDERS

A contravention of a prohibition order, or any action contributing to a contravention or an attempted contravention will not constitute a criminal offence but a civil action can be brought in respect of any contravention or apprehended contravention. The Crown can seek an injunction (or in Scotland, an interdict) prohibiting any action constituting such a contravention. Comparable provisions are found in the Fair Trading Act 1973, ss. 90 (1), (2), 93. The Secretary of State, if he believed a person to be acting in a manner contrary to a prohibition order, could seek an injunction from the Court preventing him from so doing. Any actions taken in the face of such an injunction would amount to contempt of court, thus making the person guilty of the contempt liable to committal to prison. **[169]**

It is worth recalling that the Government can call upon at least two other means of preventing an undesirable foreign takeover of a British undertaking. The Secretary of State may refer a proposed merger to the Monopolies and Mergers Commission under the powers contained in Part V of the Fair Trading Act 1973. Comparable powers under earlier legislation were invoked to investigate the proposed merger between the Dental Manufacturing Co. Ltd. or the Dentists' Supply Co. of New York and the Amalgamated Dental Co. Ltd (HC 147 of 1966). In this case the majority of the Commission approved of the merger but the delay did enable the United Kingdom company to fight off the bid. **[170]**

Secondly, the Government possesses certain powers relating to exchange control which can effectively prevent the foreign takeover of a British undertaking. Control is secured through the Exchange Control Act 1947. The rules for inward direct investment through a United Kingdom subsidiary are found in Notices EC4 and EC18; the policy is described in Bank of England, A Guide to United Kingdom Exchange Control, July, 1973. The criteria to be satisfied are primarily financial but ". . . if a non-resident wished to acquire a substantial interest in an existing United Kingdom company whose operations were regarded by H M Government as being of vital concern to the United Kingdom's economy . . . special consideration would therefore be given to an investment of this nature". Occasionally, the Government has threatened to exercise its powers as a means of extracting certain undertakings from the foreign concern. In return for the granting of exchange control permission in respect of the Chrysler Corporation's bid to control the Rootes Motor Company, Chrysler undertook, *inter alia*, to maintain a majority of British directors on the board, to expand output, particularly in assisted areas, and to permit the I.R.C. a nominee on the board (739 HC Deb. of 1966–67, col. 34; see also the White Paper on the proposed purchase of the Trinidad Oil Company by the Texas Oil Co., Cmnd. 9790 (1956)). But to rely on such a practice to control "undesirable" foreign takeovers might, first, be inefficient, particularly in relation to British undertakings already in foreign hands and sought by other, less "desirable" foreign purchasers; and, secondly, unsatisfactory because it permits a much lesser degree of Parliamentary accountability. **[171]**

Part 11 of the Industry Act 1975 mirrors comparable legislation abroad with regard to the control of multinational enterprises. In Canada, the Foreign Investment Review Act became law on 12th December 1973. This Act regulates the takeover of Canadian assets by foreigners; it also restricts the establishment of new businesses by foreigners and the development of established foreign concerns in new areas (see P. R. Hayden and J. H. Burns (1975) J.B.L. 75, 98, 174). The Australian Government has also introduced the Foreign Takeovers Act 1975 which extends existing controls to include the takeover of assets, other than shares (such as mining rights), and transfers from one foreign owner to another. Other countries have resorted to less formal means of dissuasion: in France, a major multinational electrical contractor voluntarily divested itself of a majority holding in a French company in order to be considered for a substantial Government contract. **[172]**

VESTING ORDERS

The making of a vesting order is a reserve power which will only be used "if unforeseeable developments of compelling urgency were to arise". An order can only be made when the Secretary of State is satisfied that it is necessary in the national interest and that interest cannot appropriately be protected otherwise (s. 13 (3)). The power to prohibit changes of control which would be contrary to the national interest provides the Secretary of State with a means of halting the acquisition of an important manufacturing undertaking by foreign interests. This affords an opportunity, after the prohibition order has been made, for the Government to investigate how the company which has been threatened might receive financial support if this is required, perhaps through the N.E.B. There will, nevertheless, be situations where a prohibition order will be ineffective, when, for example, a foreign company, established abroad but having U.K. subsidiaries, passes into the control of a second, foreign, company established abroad. The transactions which led to or constituted such a change of control would have taken place outside the jurisdiction and thus beyond the reach of a prohibition order. [173]

The conditions which must apply before the Secretary of State, may, with the approval of the Treasury, make an order vesting all or any of the assets comprised in an important manufacturing undertaking or the share or loan capital of any body corporate carrying on such an undertaking, in himself or in the N.E.B. are set out in s. 13 (2). An order may be made (i) if both the conditions outlined in s. 13 (1) obtain (they must, of course, be satisfied if a prohibition order is required); (ii) a prohibition order has been made within three months of laying the vesting order before Parliament; or (iii) within three months of the Secretary of State learning of circumstances that he believes constitute a change of control which has occurred since 1st February 1975, and if he believes the change of control to be contrary to the interests of the United Kingdom or of any substantial part (ss. 13 (2), 15 (4)). In each of the first two situations the Government will almost always be justified in seeking a vesting order if, in the absence of alternative sources of capital, the company will fail. The third situation is designed to prevent attempts to circumvent the Act's powers through stealth. A prohibition order cannot be used to prevent what has already happened, and if the change of control is undesirable a vesting order can be used in the absence of any alternative strategy, to safeguard the business. The restriction to changes after 1st February 1975 is designed to confine the Secretary of State's powers to changes of control occurring *after* the Bill's publication (though *before* its enactment) and thus to prevent the Bill applying to things done before those affected could have been aware of its provisions. On a day specified in the vesting order *either* the share capital of the "relevant body corporate" plus all or some of the loan capital, *or* any assets of the undertaking, will vest in the Secretary of State or in the N.E.B. or in nominees for the Board or himself. As with prohibition orders he may also make any incidental or supplementary provisions as appear to him to be necessary or expedient. [174]

A "relevant body corporate" is defined as a body corporate incorporated in the United Kingdom, the business of which, in so far as it is located in the United Kingdom, is substantially that of an important manufacturing undertaking. The definition is extended to include a holding company incorporated in the United Kingdom, of a group of companies, with the same characteristics (as the above mentioned important manufacturing undertaking) where, in addition, the Secretary of State thinks there is a serious and immediate probability of a change of control or something occurring which might lead it or where he has learnt of circumstances relating to the company which appear to him to constitute a change of control on or after 1st February 1975 (s. 13 (5), (6)). [**175**]

Two points are important in relation to this definition: first, it relates to companies incorporated in the United Kingdom only. If, therefore, an American company trading though not incorporated in the United Kingdom satisfied the conditions for a vesting order to be made, the American share capital would remain untouched but the assets of the company within the United Kingdom could be vested. Secondly, there is no question of the shares of a holding company being vested simply because it controls, as a small part of its business, an important manufacturing undertaking. It is likely that the power to vest will be exercised only if the important manufacturing undertaking accounts for a major part—more than half—of the activities of the company or group. [**176**]

In relation to the vesting of share and loan capital, the Secretary of State will vest all the company's share capital in himself or in the National Enterprise Board (or nominees for either) and will normally acquire loan capital which gives its owners special rights affecting the control of the company (e.g., rights of voting in particular circumstances, of converting loan stock to equity or of restricting the company's borrowings). He might, however, wish to leave some loan stock which has no special rights outstanding and either leave it as a debt of the company when acquired or charge it on the compensation which would be paid to the company under an order under s. 19. He is not required, therefore, to cause all the loan capital to vest. When the undertaking in question is not carried on by a body corporate, or did not account for more than a small part of the body corporate's business it might well be more appropriate for the Secretary of State to acquire the assets in the undertaking, rather than acquire the share capital of a company which had large interests other than in the undertaking in question. In passing, it should be noted that there is nothing to prevent the N.E.B., after receiving property under a vesting order, passing it on to either the Scottish or Welsh Development Agency if the property was originally vested to protect Scottish or Welsh interests. [**177**]

THE CONTENTS OF A VESTING ORDER

The scope of vesting orders is defined in s. 16. This section specifies the provisions that may be made in respect of the share capital or assets to be acquired, and the provisions that may be made to safeguard the capital or assets which are subject to a vesting order. There are no comparable provisions for prohibition orders, which merely prohibit a particular transfer. Section 16 (1) gives the Secretary of State the power in a vesting order to make provisions by which rights, liabilities or incumbrances, to which assets or capital which will vest by virtue of the order, are subject, may be:

(a) extinguished in return for compensation under s. 19;
(b) transferred to him or to the Board; or
(c) will be charged on the compensation under section 19.

An example of *rights* that might be attached to shares or assets is to be found when these are held on trust, i.e. the beneficiaries of the trust have rights in respect of the property held on their behalf by the trustee. In these circumstances the property acquired would be held by the Secretary of State free from the trust, which would attach to the compensation paid for the assets which had previously been held on trust. [**178**]

Where assets of an undertaking are subject to *liabilities* they can be dealt with in one of three ways. In a case where the Secretary of State wishes the liabilities to continue to attach to the assets in his hands, he will cause the liabilities to be transferred to him under s. 16 (1) (*b*) and the sum of compensation paid for the assets under s. 19 will accordingly equal the value of the assets minus the amount of the liabilities transferred. Where, however, the Secretary of State wishes the assets to vest in him or the N.E.B. free of liabilities, he may transfer the assets and leave the liabilities referable to them as liabilities of the person from whom the assets were transferred. In this case the compensation paid in respect of the assets would equal their full value, thus enabling their previous owner to discharge the liabilities which previously attached to them. As an alternative in this latter case, the Secretary of State may transfer assets to himself or to the N.E.B. free of liabilities (which thus remain liabilities of the previous owner of the assets), extinguish the liabilities in the hands of that previous owner and pay compensation equal to the amount of the liability to the person to whom the liability was owed. In this event the compensation paid to the previous owner of the assets will be reduced by the amount of the extinguished liabilities. [**179**]

Encumbrances will be treated in one of the three ways which were appropriate for liabilities. The freeing of assets and securities from encumbrances is a common provision in nationalisation measures so that, for example, stock certificates that have been mortgaged as security for a loan may be taken into public ownership free from the mortgage which is transferred to the Government stock issued or to the money paid as compensation. [**180**]

Examples of the transfer of rights, liabilities and encumbrances, or their charging to compensation are found in nationalisation statutes: the Iron and Steel Act 1967, s. 9 (1), and the Iron and Steel Act 1949, s. 11 (now consolidated into the Iron and Steel Act 1975) provide for the transfer of assets free from all encumbrances. An example of a provision for the transfer of property with liabilities attached is found in s. 7 of the Coal Industry Nationalisation Act 1946. No specific provision exists in nationalisation statutes to *extinguish* encumbrances and liabilities in the way possible under this section: there may be situations where it is preferable to extinguish these rather than to charge them to compensation. For example, a short-term loan could become repayable before there has been sufficient time to go through formalities, that may be complex, to transfer it; or before compensation has been assessed and paid. In both cases, it would be easier to pay off the loan, thus extinguishing it, rather than waiting for compensation. [**181**]

49

SAFEGUARDING PROVISIONS

In common with past nationalisation statutes, the Industry Act 1975 contains "safeguarding" provisions preventing the disposal of the assets of the undertaking destined for public ownership (see, for example, ss. 20 *et seq.* of the Iron and Steel Act 1949 as revised by the Iron and Steel Act 1967). Such provisions are judged necessary in order to ensure that companies do not frustrate Parliament's intentions by, for example, transferring businesses to newly formed companies, or by changing the structure of a group, or by selling assets at prices which do not reflect their true value. Particular matters to which safeguards might apply are described in s. 16 (3). General matters for which an order might make provision include the power to limit the amount of interest on loans and dividends on share capital which a company may pay; or the power to seek compensation from directors for any unnecessary or imprudent transactions conferring benefit on a person at the company's expense (for comparable powers, see ss. 18, 24 and 25 of the Iron and Steel Act 1949, as revised and amended by the 1967 Act). **[182]**

A vesting order which provides for the vesting of assets employed in an undertaking may prohibit or set aside any *transfer* of assets so employed or of any *right* in respect of such assets (s. 16 (2)). The power of the Secretary of State or the N.E.B. to recover assets which have been transferred extends to transfers made after the Secretary of State has served notice on the person carrying on the undertaking (i.e. before the draft of the order is laid before Parliament (s. 16 (4) (7)). Prospective purchasers of assets subject to a vesting order containing provisions prohibiting their transfer are put on alert by the publication of the notice in the *London Gazette*, the *Edinburgh Gazette* and the *Belfast Gazette*, as soon as practicable after the Secretary of State has served it (s. 16 (9)). The reference to the transfer of "any right" in respect of assets embraces the mortgaging or leasing of property, which, together with direct sales, comprise the most obvious ways of evading the compulsory acquisition order (see ss. 23, 24 (4) of the Iron and Steel Act 1949). **[183]**

A vesting order may include any provision that the Secretary of State considers necessary or expedient to safeguard both the capital and any assets of the company whose capital will so vest. These safeguarding provisions may extend to the assets of any subsidiary (whether wholly-owned or not) of the company whose capital will vest (s. 16 (3)). The Bill, as originally presented to Parliament, did not empower the Secretary of State to safeguard the assets of non-wholly owned subsidiaries. An amendment on the Report adopted the precedent established by s. 22 of the Iron and Steel Act 1967 because it was feared that assets which might be critical to the survival of an important manufacturing undertaking would be transferred to non-wholly owned subsidiaries and subsequently disposed of. Aggrieved minority shareholders have the right to petition a Joint Committee of the Houses of Parliament which may, if necessary, change the terms of the compensation order in their favour (para. **[188]**, *post*). **[184]**

Certain difficulties arise regarding the transfer of assets which are or will be subject to a vesting order. There is an important distinction to be made between the safeguarding of the assets of a company the shares of which are to be vested and the safeguarding of assets which are themselves assets subject to a vesting order. In respect of the latter, the Secretary of State or the N.E.B. can effect recovery or be compensated in respect of the transfer (s. 16 (6)). Furthermore, in view of the fact that a vesting order covering assets which are employed in an undertaking is absolutely limited to assets employed in the United Kingdom, there is no question of the Government or the N.E.B. seeking to recover disposed assets in foreign courts. But a company may own assets— in the form of physical assets or shares in other companies—both in the United Kingdom and overseas, and these assets may be the subject of a vesting order (s. 16 (3) (*b*)). In respect of corporate assets which have been disposed of the "important manufacturing undertaking" (or, if they are the assets of a subsidiary, its subsidiary) is entitled to recover the assets transferred, and the company will have a right to be compensated in respect of the transfer (s. 16 (5), (6)). The compensation would be claimed from the directors of the company which had improperly divested itself of assets. It seems, therefore, that if company A sold assets subject to a vesting order, to company B and this company resold them to company C, the first transaction would be set aside and all subsequent transfers would have no effect. Each party would be able to recover any money which had passed in subsequent transfers. However, neither the transferor company nor the Government acting as its owner can secure compensation from anyone who was not a party to the first transaction. The ability of the company, or the Government acting on its behalf, to set aside a transaction for the sale of "safeguarded" assets situated abroad, is open to doubt. But notwithstanding this intricate question of international law, compensation will normally be recoverable from the peccant directors for the damage caused to the company. [**185**]

MINORITY PROTECTION

Where a vesting order vests 30% or more, but not all, of the shares of a company the remaining shareholders are offered the opportunity to have their shares acquired under the vesting order (s. 14). This reflects the Government's undertaking to observe the principles of the City Code on Takeovers and Mergers, particularly Rule 34, which states that when a bid is made and accepted for 30% of a company's shares an offer must be made on the same terms for the remaining shares. [**186**]

Once 30% or more of the share capital of the company vests in the Secretary of State or the Board by virtue of a vesting order the Secretary of State must serve a notice on the holders of all the share capital and all who, to his knowledge, have a present or prospective right to subscribe for share capital, informing them of the vesting order and of the right of each of them to require the order to extend to the share capital or rights held by him. The Secretary of State must serve this notice within twenty-eight days of the making of the order (s. 14 (1)). The recipient may, within three months of the date of the notice, serve a counter-notice on the Secretary of State requiring the order to extend to his share capital or rights in the company, and from the date of the counter-notice, the vesting order will have the same effect as if the share capital on rights specified in the notice had been specified in the original vesting order (s. 14 (2), (3)). [**187**]

PARLIAMENTARY CONTROL OF VESTING ORDERS

Unlike a prohibition order, a vesting order cannot be made unless it has first been approved in draft by an Affirmative Resolution of both Houses. In common with prohibition orders, the original Bill made no provision for subjecting a vesting order to the hybrid procedure. Since the Industry Bill was published, however, the Offshore Petroleum Development (Scotland) Act 1975 has been passed which provides for a special "expedited" hybrid procedure, to be completed within twenty-eight days. The Standing Orders of the Lords have been amended to make this possible through the substitution of Standing Order 216A (Expedited hybrid instruments). This new shortened hybrid procedure will apply to vesting orders, but as already stated, prohibition orders will be subject to the full procedure.   [**188**]

COMPENSATION ORDERS—SUMMARY

The procedure for making arrangements for compensation for the acquisition of securities or assets acquired by the Government, or the extinguishment or transfer of rights, liabilities or encumbrances, under the compulsory acquisition procedure are set out in s. 19. It ties the acquisition of the securities or assets and associated transfer or extinguishment of rights, liabilities or encumbrances, to compensation by requiring that no vesting order can be made under s. 13 until an order has been laid before Parliament under s. 19 (a "compensation order") providing for compensation to be paid for the acquisition. The order dealing with compensation is to be subject to special Parliamentary procedure, as provided for in the Statutory Orders (Special Procedure) Acts 1945 and 1965. The compensation order must identify who will receive compensation and the terms of compensation, which may include arbitration; it must specify how this will be paid, which may be either in cash or through the issue of Government Stock and must make provision for interest to be paid on compensation between the date of vesting and the date of paying compensation. The order may also make different provisions in respect of different classes of capital or assets, may make provision for arbitration, and may contain additional provisions. The Statutory Orders (Special Procedure) Act 1945 is amended in its application to a compensation order to ensure that the Secretary of State is unable to withdraw an order laid under s. 19.   [**189**]

By way of contrast, no compensation is payable to anyone who suffers loss as a consequence of a prohibition order. This is partly a consequence of a difference in principle between prohibiting a particular transaction and vesting a company or assets, and partly a reflection of the practical difficulties associated with assessing losses attributable to a prohibition order. Equally it maintains the policy adopted in s. 74 of the Fair Trading Act 1973—where no compensation for the effects of a "stop notice" is payable.   [**190**]

The Secretary of State is required, before completing the first part of the two stage acquisition and compensation procedure, to have initiated the second part, providing for compensation to be paid in respect of the acquisition of the securities or assets. No order can be made to vest securities or assets in the Secretary of State or the N.E.B. under s. 13 before an order providing for compensation in respect of the acquisition or transfer of rights has been laid before both Houses of Parliament. Vesting orders are subject to Affirmative Resolution procedure, and so it will in theory be possible for a vesting order to be debated before a compensation order is laid. The purpose of this provision is thus to ensure that the compensation procedure is initiated before a vesting order is made. But it is not necessary that the compensation order should be available for discussion when the vesting order is debated in Parliament, although this would clearly be preferable (s. 19 (1)). [191]

The compensation order is subject to special Parliamentary procedure under the Statutory Orders (Special Procedure) Act 1945 as amended by the Statutory Orders (Special Procedure) Act 1965 (s. 19 (2)). The main features of the Acts are as follows:

(i) At least three days before laying an order before Parliament, the Minister must publish an announcement in *The London Gazette* of his intention of doing so (s. 2);

(ii) The order must be laid before both Houses of Parliament, and petitions may be presented within twenty-one days to amend or annul the order that has been laid (s. 3, as amended by the 1965 Act);

(iii) Petitions so made are examined jointly by the Lord Chairman of Committees in the House of Lords and by the Chairman of Ways and Means in the House of Commons (s. 3, as similarly amended);

(iv) After jointly examining any petitions, the Chairmen make a joint report to both Houses, and either House may annul the order, in which case a new order may be laid (s. 4). If there are neither petitions nor annulment, the order stands, but if there are petitions and the order is not annulled, a Joint Committee of both Houses is set up to consider petitions. Under the Standing Orders of each House, the Joint Committee consists of six members, three from each House, and is concerned to consider the petitions rather than the order itself. Petititoners may be represented by Counsel and may call witnesses; Counsel for the Minister may oppose a petition, and may call witnesses. The petitioners have a right of reply. The Committee can award costs.

(v) The Joint Committee, after considering petitions, can amend the order, or report that the order should not be approved, and its report is laid before each House (s. 5);

(vi) Unless there are Government objections, the order, as amended, then takes effect. The Minister, however, if he considers it "inexpedient that the order should take effect" in the form amended by the Joint Committee, may submit a Bill to Parliament for further consideration of the order as amended by the Joint Committee. Such a Bill would not be subject to hybrid procedure, and would be treated as if it had reached Report Stage in each House (s. 6). [192]

The effect of this special procedure is to preserve the right of individuals to petition in respect of the terms of compensation offered in return for the compulsory acquisition of securities or assets under s. 13. In addition, it requires a full measure of Parliamentary approval for the terms of compensation and combines this with a means of proceeding by Statutory Instrument that is more rapid than the introduction of a Bill, and therefore more suited to the circumstances of an urgent threat with which the powers of s. 13 are concerned. [193]

The principal Acts containing provision for the use of the special Parliamentary procedures mainly relate to cases involving compulsory acquisition, and include the Water Act 1945, the Town and Country Planning Act 1947, the Transport Act 1962 and the Pipe-lines Act 1962. Powers under the Housing Acts for compulsory purchase in respect of common, open spaces and allotments may also be exercised through the Special Parliamentary procedure. The Statutory Orders (Special Procedure) Acts do not normally apply to Northern Ireland, so s. 39 (4) extends them to Northern Ireland for the purpose of the Act. [**194**]

THE CONTENTS OF A COMPENSATION ORDER

The scope of the order dealing with compensation is designed in s. 19 (3). It *requires* the order to:

(i) identify the persons or classes of persons who will receive compensation, and to state their rights and duties, in relation to compensation (s. 19 (3) (*a*));

(ii) state how the compensation will be paid (s. 19 (3) (*b*)); and

(iii) provide for the payment of interest on compensation in respect of the "relevant period", which is defined, in relation to capital or assets, as the period commencing with the date on which the capital or assets vest in the Secretary of State or in the N.E.B. (or nominees for either) and ending with the date of payment of compensation; in relation to rights, liabilities and encumbrances, the period commencing with the date on which they are extinguished and ending on the date of payment (s. 19 (3) (*c*), (*e*) (i) (ii));

The order *may* also make provisions

(iv) for different treatment in relation to different descriptions of capital or assets and different rights, liabilities or encumbrances (s. 19 (3) (*d*)); and

(v) for the making of incidental or supplementary provisions, which may include a requirement that any dispute should be determined by recourse to arbitration (ss. 19 (3) (*e*); 20 (3) (*a*)). [**195**]

The scope of the order leaves the Secretary of State with discretion to decide on the most appropriate basis for compensation; the sub-section does not define what this basis should be. This discretion is judged necessary because of the wide range of securities and assets which may in theory be subject to the operation of the powers under s. 13. In the past the Government have used various bases for compensation, most commonly share values (railways, gas, electricity and steel), but other methods here included net maintainable revenue (Bank of England and coal), and asset valuation (road haulage and allocation of coal compensation). The Government felt that a mechanical formula leading to compensation (i.e. one of stock market valuation, net asset valuation, a multiple of past profits or earnings per share and so forth) would be unnecessarily restrictive. [**196**]

The effect of the provisions in the order are as follows: s. 19 (3) (*a*) will require the persons or classes of persons to receive compensation to be specified in an order and their amounts and duties in respect of it to be set out. The amount of compensation will be provided for under the basic provision of s. 19 (1), that the order is to provide for the payment of compensation. This would cover the method of computation and the amount. This paragraph enables provision to be made ensuring for example that rights against property taken over by a vesting order can survive as rights against compensation moneys; similarly the obligation of a trustee to property taken over will survive as obligations over compensation moneys. [**197**]

Section 19 (3) (*b*) requires the order to specify how compensation would be paid. The alternatives, set out in s. 19 (4), are by cash payments or by the issue of gilt edged stock. Compensation is payable by one or both of the means specified, and is at the discretion of the Secretary of State (subject to the procedure which has been outlined) and not at the election of the shareholder in the company subject to vesting. The most frequent method used in the past has been the issue of Government stock for major nationalisation measures. Provision has also been made for smaller payments to be in cash. Thus for road haulage, for example, British Transport 3% guaranteed stock was issued, but provision was made for cash payments not exceeding £20,000 to any person to whom not more than £20,000 was due. For the purchase of assets, payment in cash has also occurred: Rolls-Royce (1971) Ltd. purchased assets from the old company from the Receiver for a figure in excess of £85m in cash. [**198**]

A significant change is *planned* in the application of capital gains tax affecting shareholders in companies subject to vesting orders (and shareholders in shipbuilding and aircraft companies subject to nationalisation). [**199**]

Where the compensation is paid in cash, any gain on disposal is chargeable to capital gains tax and any loss qualifies for relief at the time of the disposal. Where compensation is paid by the issue of Government stock, the Finance Act 1965, Sch. 7, para. 5 provides that shareholders shall not be liable to tax on capital gains nor entitled to relief in respect of any losses arising on the occasion when they exchange their existing holdings for Government stock. Instead they are deemed to have acquired the stock at the same time and at the same cost as their existing holdings. Gains and losses accruing on the disposal of Government stock are outside the scope of capital gains tax unless a disposal takes place within twelve months of acquisition. Under the existing rules, therefore, where a shareholder is compensated by the issue of Government stock and subsequently sells the stock, any net gain or net loss on the shares or stock would be left out of account for capital gains tax unless the combined period of ownership of the shares and the Government stock was less than twelve months. [**200**]

The Finance Act 1976, s. 53 provides that where the compensation is paid by the issue of Government stock, any gains which have accrued on an existing holding of shares will be assessed when the Government stock is disposed of and any losses will similarly be available for relief. In addition, any gain or loss on the Government stock itself will be within the scope of capital gains tax until that stock has itself been held for more than twelve months. [**201**]

Section 19 (3) (*c*) requires the order to provide for interest to be paid on compensation to cover the period between the vesting of the securities or assets and the payment of compensation, or from the date on which rights, liabilities and encumbrances are extinguished to the date of compensation. Other nationalisation measures (e.g. Iron and Steel Act 1949, Sch. 4, as revised by the 1967 Act) have made comparable provision. It is particularly necessary in this

Act since the arrangements for the compensation terms to be settled after vesting are likely to result in a considerable time elapsing between the vesting of the shares or assets under s. 13 and the final payment of compensation at the end of the special Parliamentary procedure, with petitioning, under this section. Interest in the past has been paid at the rate of interest on Treasury stock when compensation was to be paid in such stock, or at the higher of 1% above Bank Rate or a fixed interest rate. The order would make provision for interest to be paid in a manner "appropriate for the circumstances of a particular acquisition". [**202**]

Section 19 (3) (*d*) enables the Secretary of State to make different provision in respect of different classes of shares (e.g. between preference and ordinary stock or between quoted and unquoted securities); or to draw a distinction between assets which are to be valued on one basis and those more appropriately valued by a second approach; or to differentiate between liabilities which have been transferred with assets as part of a business and those which have been extinguished, and for which compensation would be provided. [**203**]

Section 19 (3) (*e*) enables the Secretary of State to make incidental or supplementary provisions. It might be necessary, for example, to make provision to meet the expenses incurred by those qualifying for compensation in demonstrating their compensation rights; or to define, for the purpose of the order, what is meant by particular phrases in the order. [**204**]

Lastly, the Secretary of State is prevented from withdrawing an order dealing with compensation (s. 19 (5)). This amends the Statutory Orders (Special Procedure) Act 1945. Under s. 6 (2) of the 1945 Act the Minister, if he "considers it inexpedient" that the order as amended by the joint committee should take effect, may either withdraw it or introduce a Bill. It would clearly be wrong for the Secretary of State, if he objected to the amendments made to a compensation order by the joint committee, to withdraw the order, since this would leave the owners of the securities or assets now vested in him or the N.E.B. without compensation. It will, however, still be open to the Secretary of State, if he considers the committee's amendments unacceptable to introduce a Bill to use the alternative procedure of s. 6 of the 1945 Act which will remain. This is to proceed with the order as if it were a Public Bill which has been amended in committee. The Minister would therefore be able to negative such of the amendments as the Government thought fit on Report. [**205**]

ARBITRATION

Provision is made in the Act for the establishment of a tribunal, which will be a court of record and will have an official seal which will be judicially noted (2. 20 (1), Sch. 3, para. 1). Any dispute arising out of a vesting order or a compensation order to which one of the parties is the Secretary of State, the Board or a company, the whole or part of whose share capital has vested in either of them by virtue of the order, may be referred to the tribunal provided that no proceedings related to it have been commenced in any court. One party has simply to serve a notice on the other party or parties to the dispute, that he wishes the dispute to be determined by arbitration. In addition, the provisions of the compensation or vesting order may require the dispute to be submitted to arbitration (s. 20 (3) (*a*), (*b*)). It is envisaged that the Joint Committee will determine the policy to be adopted regarding compensation orders and the tribunal, when called upon, will deal with disputes surrounding factual matters, e.g. the value of unquoted securities (as in the nationalisation of gas, iron and steel) or of assets transferred (as in coal nationalisation), or the rights of a person to compensation. There is nothing to prevent the question of compensation going to arbitration but this can hardly have been the Government's intention. Other factual matters relating to the safeguarding provisions of s. 16, whether for example a particular transaction was such as to fall within s. 16 (3), might be referred to arbitration. Arbitration might also determine the net loss to the undertaking or company taken into public ownership. It is common for nationalisation measures to provide for a tribunal to arbitrate on matters of this sort (Iron and Steel Act 1949, s. 43, Coal Industry Nationalisation Act 1946, s. 61). An appeal lies to the Court of Appeal on any question of law or *fact* from any determination or order of the tribunal with respect to compensation under s. 16 (6). [**206**]

The composition, method of appointment, guidelines for procedure and other matters relating to the tribunal are described in Schedule 3. [**207**]

RIGHT OF ESTABLISHMENT

It might be appropriate to conclude with a reference to the ways in which the United Kingdom's membership of the European Communities affects the exercise of powers under Part II of the Act. [**208**]

Articles 52–58 of the Treaty of Rome are devoted to the "Right of Establishment". Article 52 reads thus:

"Within the framework of the provisions set out below, restrictions on the freedom of establishment of nationals of a Member State in the territory of another Member State shall be abolished by progressive stages in the course of the transitional period. Such progressive abolition shall also apply to restrictions on the setting up of agencies, branches or subsidiaries by nationals of any Member State established in the territory of any Member State.

"Freedom of establishment shall include the right to take up and pursue activities as self-employed persons and to set up and manage undertakings, in particular companies or firms within the meaning of the second paragraph of Article 58, under the conditions laid down for its own nationals by the law of the country where such establishment is effected, subject to the provisions of the Chapter relating to capital."

The Article seeks to prohibit discrimination based upon nationality. [**209**]

Article 58 amplifies who are to be the beneficiaries to this right of establishment:

"Companies or firms formed in accordance with the law of a Member State and having their registered office, central administration or principal place of business within the Community shall, for the purpose of this Chapter, be treated in the same way as natural persons who are nationals of Member States.

" 'Companies or firms' means companies or firms constituted under civil or commercial law, including cooperative societies, and other legal persons governed by public or private law, save for those which are non-profit-making."

The definition embraces three tests of nationality and incorporation: ". . . companies or firms formed in accordance with the law of a Member State and having their registered office (*siège statutaire*), central administration or principal place of business within the Community . . ." As drafted there would be little to prevent a non-Community national from establishing a nominee company with a registered office in a Member State in order to seek the benefit of the right of establishment. Fortunately, the definition is informally restricted by the Convention of the Mutual Recognition of Companies and Bodies Corporate of February 1968 (Suppl. to Bulletin 2, 1969) and the General Programme on the Freedom of Establishment (J.O. 1962, 36). The latter states (Title I) that where a company has *only* a registered office within the E.E.C. its activities must have an *effective* and *continuous* link with the economy of the Member State if it is to benefit from the right of establishment.   [**210**]

By virtue of s. 2 (4) of the European Communities Act 1972 (A.L.S. Vol. 205), Part II of the Industry Act 1975 must be read subject to the Treaties establishing the European Communities. The provisions relating to the right of establishment in the Treaty of Rome affect Part II of the Act, and in fact, following the judgment of the European Court in Case 2/74 *Reyners* v. *Belgian State*, [1974] E.C.R. 631; [1974] 2 C.M.L.R. 305, are directly applicable.   [**211**] The view of the Government, however, is somewhat different.

". . . Our legal advice is that the acquisition of property by one member state by a national of another does not fall within the freedom of establishment when the acquisition is being attempted from outside the member state in which the property is situated . . .

"It would therefore be no infringement of the right of freedom of establishment for a prohibition or vesting order to be made to prevent or frustrate a bid for a U.K. company made by a company registered in a member state—that is, a takeover bid from abroad—but it would infringe our community obligations if we prevented a U.K. subsidiary of a company registered in and controlled by residents of a member state from acquiring a British concern through these powers which could not by their nature be used to prevent acquisition of a British company which was not foreign controlled . . .

"If therefore, an E.E.C. company organised a bid for a key British manufacturing undertaking through a U.K. subsidiary, cl. 9–13 [corresponding to ss. 11–20] could not be applied to prevent or frustrate the acquisition without the U.K. breaching its obligations . . . it would not be in breach of our E.E.C. obligations to prevent the acquisition of key British manufacturing enterprises by companies which are themselves controlled by non-E.E.C. residents provided that the prohibition applies equally, no matter whether the acquiring company was a U.K. company or a company of any other member state . . . such action would not discriminate between British and other E.E.C. companies but would rather be an action applying to companies in all E.E.C. member states which were controlled by non-E.E.C. residents. Thus it would not be possible for a bid by a non-E.E.C. acquirer to evade our legislation by being routed through a non-E.E.C. subsidiary even if that non-E.E.C. subsidiary were an established company . . ." 894 HC Deb., col. 1397–8, Mr. Kaufman. [**212**]

This cannot be correct. Article 52 is designed to eliminate discrimination between undertakings of the host country and undertakings based in other Member States not, as the extract seems to imply, to treat undertakings from other Members States in a way comparable to non-Community undertakings. If, therefore, and subject to the above mentioned caveat regarding the company's "effective and continuous link" with the Member State, an enterprise to which art. 58 applied was faced with a prohibition and/or a vesting order this would be a contravention of the United Kingdom's treaty obligations and, moreover, could be challenged by the undertaking in question. [**213**]

CHAPTER 5
PLANNING AGREEMENTS

After the National Enterprise Board the second major instrument of policy found in the Industry Act 1975 is the Planning Agreement. A Government Minister described such an agreement as ". . . essentially the development of a relationship between two sides, which is partly based on finance but, perhaps more important, on the exchange of information and understanding about the intentions of each side." Planning Agreements emerged from the work of the Ministry of Technology in 1970, though it could reasonably be argued that the industrial investment schemes created under the Industrial Expansion Act 1968 constituted an early form of "planning agreement". The French have long adopted the "contractual technique" in economic planning, whereby the Government directed particular activities by conferring Government benefits in exchange for desired conduct on the part of companies, and trade associations. Companies were expected to make a formal commitment to modernise or eliminate inefficient plant. In return, the Government permitted selective tax concessions, granted certain subsidies or allowed a relaxation of price controls. There is little doubt that the French experience lies behind Part III of the Act. [**214**]

As envisaged in 1970 Planning Agreements possessed a number of characteristics, which though not present in the 1975 Act, merit comment here as placing the final formulation in better focus. First, planning agreements were coercive in character. They were to be the conduit along which all forms of Government aid flowed. Secondly the trade unions were to play a significant, direct role in the drafting of the agreement, and in order to allow them to do so effectively the company in question was to be required to furnish the union with the necessary information. Disclosure of information, both to Government in the interests of economic planning, and to the trade unions, was seen as an essential concomitant to Planning Agreements. The political evolution of the Industry Act revealed the strong feelings engendered by the association of Planning Agreements with all forms of state aids and of disclosure of information, and, as is evident from the structure of the Act, *compulsory* disclosure is divorced from the agreements themselves. [**215**]

A planning agreement is defined as ". . . a voluntary arrangement as to the strategic plans of a body corporate for the future development in the United Kingdom over a specified period of an undertaking of the body corporate or of one or more of that body's subsidiaries, or a joint undertaking of the body corporate and one or more of its subsidiaries, being an arrangement entered into by the body corporate and any Minister of the Crown which in the opinion of that Minister is likely over the specified period to contribute significantly to national needs and objectives" (s. 21 (2)). [**216**]

The White Paper (the Regeneration of British Industry, Cmnd. 5710 (1974) at para. 11) emphasised that a Planning Agreement will not be an agreement in the sense of a civil contract enforceable at law, and there will not be any compulsion on a body corporate to enter into a Planning Agreement (but see para. [**235**], *post*). The word "strategic" was added during the Committee stage to emphasise that the Government was not concerned with the day to day decisions, but more the medium and long term plans, of the entity in question. It is envisaged that consultations will take place annually, with sufficient scope to permit the revision of agreements during the course of the year should circumstances so require. It is plain from the wording of s. 21 (2) that Planning Agreements can be forged between the Government and the nationalised industries, in addition to companies in the private sector. On the Government's side the agreement will be fashioned by the department with the most immediate interest in the plans of the other participant; for example, the Secretary of State for Industry will be responsible for Planning Agreements with companies in the machine tools industry, or the Ministry of Agriculture, Fisheries and Food for a food company. In every case the Planning Agreement will apply to enterprises only in respect of British holdings and developments within the United Kingdom. The Act is silent as to the duration of a planning agreement: the White Paper refers to a normal period of three years, though it is possible that companies would be required to provide plans on a longer timescale. The agreement itself would have the relevant time period included in it, along with further provisions relating to annual plans. No statutory limitation is placed upon the nature of the enterprise that may make a Planning Agreement: unlike other provisions of the Act it is not necessary for the company to be an "important manufacturing undertaking" nor indeed, for it to be in manufacturing at all. The only test of eligibility is the requirement that the enterprise must, in the opinion of the Minister ". . . contribute significantly to national needs and objectives". This is a test that most banks and insurance companies would easily satisfy. [**217**]

THE CONTENTS OF AN AGREEMENT

It is perhaps apparent that s. 21 is a *de minimis* section. There is no statutory guidance on what should be included in a Planning Agreement; individual items will naturally vary in importance according to the situation and nature of the company concerned. The Department of Industry's Discussion Document, "The Contents of a Planning Agreement" lists the following items, which together constitute a provisional agenda for a Planning Agreement. [**218**]

The General Background

Item 1 Economic Prospects—The Government would contribute an assessment of trends in world trade and review with the company the effects of possible change in the national economy on its future prospects. [**219**]

Item 2—The Government would request the company to provide a "substantial" note on its long term objectives, including a quantification of the important changes in the envisaged balance of company activities in the long run and the broad implications for investment, productivity, employment, exports, and product and process development. This information, which will also be garnered from other companies in the same industrial sector, will enable the Government to formulate in collaboration with its other partners in N.E.D.O., a sectoral industrial strategy.   [**220**]

The Company

Item 3 U.K. Sales—The Government will seek information on the past and future levels of:

    (i) sales for each main product line;
    (ii) the company's market share;
    (iii) the basis of the company's forecast and how they relate to any forecasts made by trade associations or by N.E.D.O.;
    (iv) the way sales are affected by Government policies and the economic climate;
    (v) in appropriate cases, the prospects for import saving.

The information so acquired is intended, in part, to facilitate Government support for specific projects which will reduce the U.K.'s demand for imports.   [**221**]

Item 4 Exports—The Government will wish to share the company's views of its export prospects, together with an indication of the company's long term objectives and marketing strategy.   [**222**]

Item 5 Investment—The level, quality and deployment of investment is central to Planning Agreement discussions. The Government will request detailed information on:

    (i) the level of investment, identifying projects of major significance and the aggregate level of investment in each of the company's divisions and major plants;
    (ii) the proportion of investment in the assisted areas;
    (iii) investment related particularly to exports or import saving where this is a specific objective;
    (iv) comparative information on investment per employee and on constraints to investment.

Flowing from this exchange of information, the agreement could embrace assistance under the Industry Act 1972, the granting of industrial development certificates, location in the assisted areas, guaranteed rates of regional development grant and other means at the disposal of the Government to encourage more efficient use of national resources.   [**223**]

Item 6 Employment and Training—The Government will wish to know the problems a company faces in such fields as recruitment, wastage and training and, in particular, redundancy. The Government will seek information on the present numbers in employment, prospective major changes and the scope for increasing employment in assisted areas. On the Government's side the information will be of value to the Department of Employment Group, in its work in Manpower Planning. The Group includes the Manpower Services Commission and its Executive Agencies, the Training Services Agency and the Employment Services Agency. Government assistance could be brought to bear in support of investment programmes and decisions on particular applications for industrial development certificates in the assisted areas. [224]

Item 7 Productivity—It is intended that the planning agreement framework should be used to identify the constraints to increases in productivity of all factors of production. [225]

Item 8 Finance—Three aspects of corporate financing are suggested as being of importance, namely the financing of the company's investment programme, meeting the effects of inflation and providing early notice of any threats to levels of employment or the continuous operation of particular plants as a result of financial stringency. [226]

Item 9 Prices Policy—The control of prices is of immediate contemporary importance. It is realised, however, that price restraint can have deleterious effects on investment and efficiency. It is possible that the Planning Agreement will be judged an appropriate means whereby selective relaxation of price controls could be secured in return for certain undertakings on the part of the company. (This was hinted at in a speech of the Secretary of State for Prices and Consumer Protection, 885 HC Deb., col. 764.) [227]

Item 10 Industrial Relations—The Government will seek discussions on the current practice of the company. [228]

Item 11 Interests of Consumers and the Community—The Act is silent about the role that consumers and local authorities may play in the creation of a Planning Agreement, but it is envisaged that in appropriate cases such interests will be consulted (para. 15 of the White Paper). [229]

Item 12 Product and Process Development—This heading will give the company the opportunity of discussing with the Government the main lines of its technological developments and the possibility of using the resources of any of the Government's Industrial Research Establishments and taking up financial support under the Science and Technology Act. The Government has an obvious interest in certain characteristics of new products; for example, a planned product may have an import-saving role, or may consume less energy resources. In both instances, it is possible that Government assistance might be available to expedite the development of the product. [230]

THE GOVERNMENT'S CONTRIBUTION

The obligations, albeit voluntarily imposed on public and private enterprises, are not inconsiderable: it is appropriate to consider what Government is giving in return. Section 21 allows the Secretary of State, when he has laid a statement before each House of Parliament that a Planning Agreement has been concluded with an undertaking, to make payment of regional development grants and give assistance under the Industry Act 1972 (Part II) on the basis of the law existing on the date of the Planning Agreement, notwithstanding changes made by Order under the Industry Act 1972 or under the Local Employment Act 1972. [231]

The Secretary of State is empowered to make payments of regional development grant in respect of approved capital expenditure on projects defined in a Planning Agreement and incurred within a period specified in the Agreement at rates which are not lower than those applying when the Agreement was concluded. The effect of this power is to enable the Secretary of State to guarantee to an undertaking that it will receive, on certain projects named in an Agreement, on expenditure within a time period and within an amount that may be specified in the Agreement, regional development grant at not less than the rates current when the Agreement was made. The power to make regional development grants is contained in Part I of the Industry Act 1972. Grants may be given in respect of approved capital expenditure (s. 1). The activities qualifying for grant and the prescribed rate of grant are set in the table in s. 1 (3). These depend on whether an activity is in a special development area, development area, or intermediate area. The guarantee will safeguard the recipient against changes that might occur between the concluding of the agreement and the incurring of expenditure through variations in the *rate of grant* under s. 3 (1) of the Industry Act 1972; through variations in the *definition of qualifying expenditure* under s. 3 (2) of the Industry Act 1972; or through variations in the *relevant geographical areas* made under ss. 1 (1), 18 (2) of the Local Employment Act 1972 and s. 1 (4) of the Industry Act 1972 (relating to the definition of intermediate, development and special development areas). He will also be able to enter into commitments to provide assistance under s. 7 of the Industry Act 1972 which gives power to provide assistance for undertakings which are wholly or mainly in assisted areas (defined as development areas, intermediate areas and Northern Ireland), since this power will continue in relation to a project specified in a Planning Agreement, notwithstanding any change in geographical areas. It is understood that no major changes are contemplated.

[**232**]

The aforementioned somewhat jejune guarantee is the sole financial incentive for an undertaking to enter into a Planning Agreement. It should be noted that there is no duty placed upon the Government to underwrite the risks attached to Government grants. Although the express purpose of the provisions of s. 21 (1) is to provide greater certainty in relation to financial assistance to Planning Agreement companies, it was judged inappropriate to eliminate the Secretary of State's discretion. The grant itself, is, of course, discretionary.

[**233**]

As earlier stated, there is no contractual basis to a Planning Agreement, it is ". . . a developing relationship between a company and the Government". The granting and continuance of the guarantee is conditional on the undertaking fulfilling its obligations under the agreement. This is not to say that the undertaking must guarantee that it performs its obligations, for the Government expressly acknowledged that market conditions might change over the course of a Planning Agreement's lifetime, and in a manner which is entirely beyond the control of the company. This would not ". . . diminish the commitment, at least on the side of the Government, to a Planning Agreement" (Standing Committee E, col. 1175, Mr. Meacher). On the other hand, the undertaking must ensure that other aspects of its performance, which lie within its powers to influence, must proceed in accordance with the terms of the Planning Agreement. On one level this merely declares that certainty in the terms of financial assistance cannot be given in a manner which bears no relation to the future actions and intentions of the undertaking. This quite acceptable proposition is fraught with problems, not least of which is the question of what constitutes "performance". There is no guidance in the Act, or elsewhere, on the conditions which will have to be satisfied before the Government is entitled to withdraw the guarantee. In Mr. Meacher's words: ". . . we are determined, so far as we can, to keep the law out of this kind of activity which is concerned with a developing relationship, not with an exchange of legal or financial benefits." (Standing Committee E, col. 1248.) [234]

Whatever the precise legal status of the obligations which may be created under a Planning Agreement, the agreements themselves are said to be voluntary in character. The White Paper, at para. 11 states "There will . . . be no statutory requirement upon a company to conclude an agreement". Doubts have been expressed that Government would seek to make the granting of certain discretionary benefits conditional on the conclusion of a Planning Agreement. The list of benefits which might be involved is formidable: financial assistance under Part II of the Industry Act 1972, Industrial Development Certificates, Office Development Permits, grants under the Local Employment Act 1972, grants made by the National Research Development Corporation under the Development of Inventions Act 1967, export credit guarantees, and contracts with Government Departments or the nationalised industries. [235]

In exercising a discretionary power, the Minister is entitled to take any relevant consideration into account. It is not unarguable that in certain circumstances (though not as an inflexible rule) the conclusion of a Planning Agreement would be an appropriate condition prior to the granting of a particular benefit. Additional pressure to enter into a Planning Agreement may be forthcoming from trade unions. It is debatable, though, whether industrial action designed to coerce an employer to enter into an agreement would be a "trade dispute" within the meaning of s. 29 of the Trade Union and Labour Relations Act 1974 (A.L.S. Vol. 222). If it is not so judged, then the immunities to actions in tort, found in s. 14, would not apply and any losses would be recoverable at the suit of the employer. [236]

THE ROLE OF THE N.E.B.

The National Enterprise Board is but one of many Government agencies which could be utilised to remedy deficiencies in industrial organisation revealed by the discussions surrounding a Planning Agreement. The White Paper, at para. 12, suggests that these discussions ". . . could help to identify requirements for investment funds for consideration by the National Enterprise Board, if necessary by means of joint ventures with the companies". But the N.E.B. will not have access to information about individual companies supplied to the Government in confidence in the context of Planning Agreements. The N.E.B. will only become involved following the consent of the company in question. It is envisaged that on occasions the N.E.B. will take the initiative with regard to the problems of a particular sector of industry, which might come to light following an assessment of information supplied by several companies. But when involving the N.E.B. the Government is under a duty to ensure that information supplied in confidence by individual companies about their affairs is withheld from the N.E.B. (Draft Guidelines, para. 26). There is no sanction, civil or criminal, following the divulging of information supplied in confidence. The Government's view was simply that the most effective guarantee of security would be the refusal of industry to give information to the Government and in the absence of compulsory powers, the system would break down.   [**237**]

CONCLUSION

The ravages of political compromise are evident in s. 21. The uneasy divorce between voluntary disclosure of information (Part III) and compulsory dis- closure (Part IV), combined with the equivocal role of trade unions combine to weaken much of the force behind the original conception. Equally, it is not clear what the relationship will be between the Department concluding a Planning Agreement and N.E.D.O. or the Economic Development Committees.

[**238**]

CHAPTER 6

DISCLOSURE OF
INFORMATION

INTRODUCTION

The disclosure provisions in the Industry Bill proved somewhat contentious. Indeed, nothing in the Bill provoked as much opposition. This was partly because much of the rationale for disclosure lay in its link with Planning Agreements, which the publication of the Bill severed. It was not obvious to many commentators why additional information should be disclosed to Government departments, still less why such information should be furnished to trade unions. The Bill was heavily amended on Report in response to concerted opposition both in and out of Parliament. [**239**]

For the purposes of the Industry Act 1975 "disclosure" consists of two separate procedures. First, the Treasury is required to maintain, make available and provide access to information contained in a computerised macro-economic model. Additional facilities are extended to corporate bodies which have entered or intend to enter Planning Agreements with a Government Department. Secondly, companies may be required in certain circumstances to divulge information on specified matters to the Government. Failure to do so without reasonable cause constitutes a criminal offence punishable by a fine. The procedure is initiated by the issue of a preliminary notice. If after three months the Minister is not satisfied that the company will voluntarily disclose the required information an Order may be laid before Parliament. On receipt of the information the Minister may require the company to pass all or some of the information on to one or more "relevant trade unions". The discretion which rests in the Minister in choosing which "relevant undertaking" should disclose information to the Government is accompanied by a further discretionary power to decide which information should be passed to the trade unions. The Government may refer to reasons of national policy or a number of "special reasons" in support of its decision not to insist that the information should be furnished to the trade unions. This discretion, in respect of the application of "special reasons" only, is reviewable by an Advisory Committee. The Minister can overrule the findings of this Committee and insist that information should be passed to trade unions, but this transfer is subject to an Order being laid before Parliament and taking effect. Any breach of confidentiality, other than those disclosures explicitly recognised by the Act, will constitute a criminal offence punishable by a fine or imprisonment or both. [**240**]

The divorce of the compulsory disclosure provisions and Planning Agreements brings into relief the different objectives that each are designed to achieve. Planning Agreements have already been described. The inclusion of compulsory disclosure is essentially a reserve power, to be used when there is no sign of voluntary disclosure. The scope of the disclosure provisions is wider than that of the purely voluntary Planning Agreements: information may be required as to how the plans of major enterprises interact within a particular industrial sector, perhaps for the purpose of sponsoring a scheme under s. 8 of the Industry Act 1972. Secondly, information could be sought from a company or companies in a sector where the Government had not, or was unwilling to conclude, a Planning Agreement. [**241**]

Information is collected under the Statistics of Trade Act 1947 but this is subject to severe restriction both within the Government and in the use to which it may be put. Information is aggregated in such a way as to explicitly conceal information relating to individual firms (s. 9). The information so collected could not be used, for example, to assess the sponsorship of a scheme of assistance under the Industry Act 1972. [**242**]

The process whereby information is furnished to trade unions under the Industry Act 1975 differs from the procedure contained in ss. 17–21 of the Employment Protection Act 1975 (A.L.S. Vol. 235) in several important respects. First, in this latter Act there is no qualification regarding the nature or importance of the enterprise which is required to furnish information. As we shall see, under the Industry Act 1975, the duty to disclose is owed by only the most substantial of concerns in *manufacturing* industry. Secondly, the nature of the information to be divulged is different: under the Employment Protection Act the employer must disclose all information in his possession which is both information without which the trade union representatives would be to a material extent impeded in carrying on collective bargaining, *and* which he should disclose for that purpose "in accordance with good industrial relations practice". The collection and dissemination of information under the Industry Act is not designed with collective bargaining in mind but for ". . . consultations between Government, employers or workers on the outlook for a particular sector of manufacturing industry, including the outlook for the major companies in that sector . . ." Thirdly, under the Employment Protection Act the trade union must take the initiative whereas under the Industry Act the Minister starts and enforces the process, although he may respond to trade union requests that information should be sought from certain companies. [**243**]

DISCLOSURE BY COMPANIES

A Minister, which for this purpose is defined to include the Secretary of State and, in recognition of the importance of food manufacturing in the economy, the Minister of Agriculture, Fisheries and Food (s. 37 (1)) may serve a "preliminary notice" on a company or companies, which will, *inter alia*, inform the undertaking that if in the event of a refusal to pass information both to the Minister and to each "relevant trade union" he will consider making an Order requiring the company or companies to do so. [**244**]

The information must be required, in the opinion of either of the Ministers ". . . to form or to further national economic policies, or needed for consultations between Government, employers or workers on the outlook for a particular sector of manufacturing industry, including the outlook for major companies in that sector . . ." (s. 28 (1)). It can only be sought from a company or group of companies which, in so far as the undertaking carries on business in the United Kingdom, is in the opinion of the Minister, wholly or mainly engaged in manufacturing industry (defined, as in s. 11 (2), by reference to s. 37 (1) (3)). The "preliminary notice" will be served either on the company carrying on the undertaking or on a group's holding company if it is registered in the United Kingdom, or on all the companies in the group if the holding company is not registered in the United Kingdom (s. 28 (2)). [245]

Two further conditions must be satisfied. It must "appear" to the Minister (i) that the undertaking makes a significant contribution to a sector (the definition of which is left to the Minister serving the notice (s. 29 (9)) of an industry important to the economy of the United Kingdom or to that of any substantial part and (ii) that it is desirable for the purpose of obtaining information of that description that the company or companies concerned should provide the Government and a representative of each relevant trade union with any such information relating to the undertaking (s. 28 (1)). [246]

It is clear, therefore, that the scope of Part IV of the Act is quite narrow. It excludes enterprises with no interest or only a peripheral interest in manufacturing industry. The condition found in s. 28 (1) (i), that the undertaking must be important in relation to a sector which is itself important to the economy, must exclude all but the largest of industrial concerns. The matter is left, however, to the discretion of the Minister, whose actions are unlikely to be inhibited by the wording of the Act. There may be political consequences, however. [247]

When the Minister serves a preliminary notice a statement must be laid before each House of Parliament, specifying the company or companies concerned, which of the two conditions in s. 28 (1) (*a*), (*b*) appear to satisfy him and the date on which the notice was served (s. 28 (3)). [248]

The preliminary notice itself must repeat which condition in s. 28 (1) (*a*), (*b*) appears to satisfy the Minister, announce his intention of laying an Order before Parliament if voluntary co-operation is not forthcoming and, thirdly, instruct the undertaking to give a "representative" of each "relevant trade union" (who then becomes an "authorised representative") a notice of the service of the preliminary notice within fourteen days of the date on which it is served. The preliminary notice will stipulate a period within which the Minister must receive a list of the "authorised representatives". [249]

A "representative" is defined as an official or other person who is authorised by a relevant trade union to carry on negotiations about one or more of the matters specified in s. 29 (1) of the Trade Union and Labour Relations Act 1974. If an "authorised representative", i.e. the recipient of a notice of service of a preliminary notice, ceases to be a representative of his "relevant trade union", or gives the company or companies concerned notice that he desires to be discharged from acting as authorised representative of that union, or ceases for any other reason to be available to act as that union's authorised representative, the company or companies concerned must inform another representative that he is to be the authorised representative of that union and request the

Minister to amend the list of authorised representatives accordingly (s. 29 (2)).
[250]

A "relevant trade union" means an independent trade union, as defined in s. 30 (1) of the Trade Union and Labour Relations Act 1974 (essentially, a trade union not under the domination, financial or otherwise, of the employer), which the company or companies concerned recognise for the purpose of negotiations about one or more of the matters specified in s. 29 (1) of that Act in relation to persons employed in the undertaking in question; or, a trade union which the Advisory Conciliation and Arbitration Service has recommended for recognition under the Employment Protection Act 1975 which is operative within the meaning of s. 15 of that Act.   [251]

After the service of the preliminary notice three months must elapse before an Order requiring the company or companies concerned to furnish the Government and relevant trade unions with the specified information can be made (s. 28 (5)). But to emphasise still further that the powers under Part IV of the Act are reserve powers, a statutory duty is placed on the Minister to satisfy himself, firstly, that the information will not voluntarily be disclosed to him and the authorised representatives of each relevant trade union and, secondly, to permit both the company or companies concerned and the trade union representatives the opportunity of making their views known to him (s. 28 (6) (7)). The Order, which is subject to the negative resolution procedure, affords the possibility of Parliamentary review of the Minister's discretion. A positive resolution procedure would, of course, subject the Order to the hybrid procedure in the Lords.   [252]

DUTY TO GIVE INFORMATION TO THE MINISTER

The Minister who has made an Order under s. 28 may specify by notice the form and content of the information he requires from the relevant undertaking. The notice may also specify a "reasonable time" within which the information should be furnished to him. The information itself can only relate to the United Kingdom interests of the relevant concern, thus repeating the undertaking of the White Paper (at para. 17) that only British holdings of multinational concerns would be covered by the legislation (s. 30 (1)). A copy of the notice must be sent to the authorised representatives of each relevant trade union (s. 30 (4)).   [253]

The matters about which information may be sought are exclusively those listed in s. 30 (2) (i.e. there is no provision comparable to that contained in s. 5 of the Statistics of Trade Act 1947 which permits the Minister to amend the Schedule to that Act):

(a) the persons employed in the undertaking, or persons normally so employed (but not specifically as to individuals). This information is also obtainable by virtue of the provisions of s. 18 of the Companies Act 1967 (A.L.S. Vol. 159). A similar restraint to the garnering of information on individuals is found in s. 18 (1) (*d*) of the Employment Protection Act 1975;

(b) the undertaking's capital expenditure;

(c) fixed capital assets used in the undertaking;

(d) any disposal or intended disposal of such assets;

(e) any acquisition or intended acquisition of fixed capital assets for use in the undertaking;

(f) the productive capacity and capacity utilisation of the undertaking;

(g) the undertaking's output and productivity;

(h) the sales of the undertaking's products;

(i) exports of those products by the undertaking. A similar requirement is to be found in s. 20 of the Companies Act 1967, where the value of the goods exported must be stated in the Directors' Report of certain companies;

(j) sales of industrial or intellectual property owned or used in connection with the undertaking, grants of rights in respect of such property, and contracts for any such sales or grants. The Act contains a caveat to this provision: it prevents a Minister from acquiring information about the *details* of know-how or of any research or development programme. This was inserted into the Bill partly as a response to the opinion that such disclosure would inhibit joint venture agreements with overseas companies. The Government is concerned not with the contents of any patent or licence but with their sale or prospective sale. "Know-how" has the same meaning assigned to it as in s. 386 (7) of the Income and Corporation Taxes Act 1970 (A.L.S. Vol. 188); "industrial or intellectual property" includes, though not exclusively, patents, designs, trade marks, know-how and copyrights (s. 30 (5), (6));

(k) expenditure on any research or development programme.

The above headings are self-explanatory. [**254**]

The notice will specify the precise form in which the information should be furnished, for example, in certain industries it is customary not to specify values but quantities or volumes. The notice may require information on any of the above items in relation to a *specified date* not earlier than the commencement of the most recently completed financial year of the person specified in the notice; information required in relation to a *period* can only be sought for a period not earlier than the commencement of that year. These provisions ensure that the powers may not be used to obtain extensive information over a long time period in the past but are confined to recent events, either on specified dates or over recent periods (s. 30 (3)). Several of the items call for a statement of future intention: this is obviously essential if they are to assist in the formation of economic planning. The power to seek estimates for the future is contained in s. 1 of the Statistics of Trade Act 1947. The requirement is here construed as a requirement only to give a forecast (s. 30 (3)). [**255**]

There is no means of appealing from the requirement to furnish information to a Minister, save the rather distant prospect of securing the annulment of the Order by either House of Parliament. [**256**]

INFORMATION FOR TRADE UNIONS

The United Kingdom legislation in respect of disclosure of information is somewhat different from foreign enactments in its two-fold insistence on selective rather than general disclosure and disclosure to trade unions rather than to the general body of employees. The White Paper (at para. 20) sought to establish a "right" that the information passed to the Minister should, subject to considerations of the national interest and serious prejudice to the company's commercial interests, be passed *in toto* to the relevant trade unions. This view was successfully opposed and the resulting compromise is enshrined in s. 31.

[257]

After the Minister has received the information specified in the notice under s. 30 he is under a duty before proceeding further, to allow the company or companies concerned and the authorised representative of each relevant trade union an opportunity of making representations to him (s. 31 (5)). After these discussions have been effected the Minister may serve a further notice on the company or companies concerned provisionally requiring them to furnish to the authorised representative of each relevant trade union the whole or part of the information which has been furnished to him.   [**258**]

The Minister is vested with a discretion to decide which information should be passed to the trade unions and this discretion must be exercised by reference to reasons of national policy or to a catalogue of "special reasons" (s. 31 (2)).

[259]

Reasons of national policy consist, first, in the consideration of whether the furnishing of the information would be undesirable in the national interest. This latter concept is no where defined and indeed, is probably indefinable. It will probably include any disclosure of information which might embarrass the Government in its dealings with other countries or reveal certain defence interests or matters which affect Government contracts. The second reason of national policy refers to the situation where information could not be disclosed by the company without contravening a prohibition imposed by or under an enactment. An example of a pre-existing statutory limitation on the disclosure of information is at present contained in s. 2 of the Official Secrets Act 1911 (s. 31 (3)). It should be noted that the Minister's decision is not susceptible to any review.   [**260**]

"Special reasons" apply if the Minister considers:

(a) that the information was communicated to the company or companies concerned in confidence or was information which they otherwise obtained in consequence of the confidence reposed in them by another person. It is clear that this paragraph covers the situation where confidentiality is imposed by contract at the time when the information is communicated. A confidence is a confidence. But a contract to keep a matter confidential would not fall within the scope of s. 31 (4) (a): if this was not so it would be an invitation to widespread evasion of the Act. A company could conclude confidentiality agreements which covered much if not all of the information that might come within the scope of the Act, merely for the purpose of evasion;

(b) that the disclosure of the information would cause substantial injury to the undertaking. This provision is not synonomous with disclosure benefiting a trade competitor. In addition, the statutory obligation to disclose information will override any contractual obligation not to do so;

(c) that its disclosure would cause substantial injury to a substantial number of employees of the undertaking (s. 31 (4)).   [**261**]

After the Minister has completed his deliberations he will present the notice under s. 31 (1) to the company or companies concerned, stating which information, if any, he proposes to require them to furnish to the trade unions. At the same time, he will send a notice to the authorised representatives stating whether or not he is requiring full disclosure on the part of the company or companies concerned. If the Minister decides that certain information should be withheld he is under a duty to give the authorised representatives ". . . such indication of the nature (without disclosing the substance) of any information which the Minister proposes should not be furnished for special reasons as will enable the representatives to consider whether or not they ought to exercise their right to require a reference under s. 32" (*post*). The notice to the undertaking must specify a reasonable period, which will not be less than twenty-eight days. This period establishes the limit within which a reference to an advisory committee must be made. If by the end of this period there has been no reference or a reference has been withdrawn the Minister may notify the undertaking and the authorised representatives of each relevant trade union that his provisional notice under s. 31 will be treated as containing his final decision (s. 32 (10), (11)).

[**262**]

THE ADVISORY COMMITTEE AND PARLIAMENTARY PROCEDURE

An undertaking which has been required by the Minister to furnish information to authorised representatives of relevant trade unions, may instruct the Minister to make a reference to an advisory committee in order to seek a recommendation releasing it from that requirement. If the Minister proposes that some or all of the information furnished to him should not be passed to trade unions, then he may refer the matter to an advisory committee or the authorised representatives of the relevant trade unions may do so (s. 32 (1)–(3)). In every case, the only question at issue is whether or not "special reasons" apply. The Minister himself is the sole judge of what constitutes reasons of national policy. The committee has no power to advise or comment upon the Minister's decision which will be taken without prejudice to any subsequent application to the committee. [**263**]

The Government's original proposal was that references should be made to the Central Arbitration Committee established under s. 10 of the Employment Protection Act 1975. The decisions of this body would have been binding on the Minister. The Government introduced amendments which place on the Minister the responsibility for deciding what information obtained under the compulsory powers should be disclosed to trade unions. In doing so, the list of considerations which the Minister would have to take into account was enlarged. It was hoped thereby to avoid the need for repeated references to the independent committee on points that may have been settled in other, analogous cases. The threat of large scale references to a committee with binding authority over the Minister might have had the effect of frustrating the information procedure. The advisory committee's role in the Act is to consider any such references and to advise the Minister on them. Before doing so the committee has to give the undertaking and the trade unions an opportunity of making representations to it (s. 32 (5)). But it is not now for the committee to make the final decision on these matters. The final decision is left for the

Minister, but only after he has received and considered the committee's report (s. 32 (7)). The Minister must notify (a) the company or companies concerned; (b) the authorised representatives of each relevant trade union; and (c) the advisory committee of his final decision. The information must then be passed on to the trade unions within the time specified by the Minister (s. 32 (8)).

[**264**]

If the Minister wishes to set aside the committee's advice and require the disclosure of information which it has advised should be withheld, he is required to make an Order, subject to the negative resolution procedure, which may not take effect until twenty-eight days from the date on which it was laid before Parliament. The Order must specify the nature but not the substance of the information to be furnished contrary to the committee's advice. It must require the information to be furnished to each relevant trade union's authorised representative within the time specified in the Order (s. 32 (13)). The advisory committee itself will be constituted from three panels of persons, drawn up by the Secretary of State with the consent of the Minister of Agriculture, Fisheries and Food, and from time to time revised. They consist of: a panel whose members have experience in industry as employers or managers; a panel whose members have experience in industrial affairs as representatives of workers; and panels whose members are barristers or solicitors, or advocates or solicitors who have practised in Scotland. The chairman will be drawn from the panel of lawyers and all members of this panel will be appointed with the consent of the Lord Chancellor or, where appropriate, the Lord-President of the Court of Session. The committee will meet in private and any breach of confidentiality with regard to its proceedings will constitute a criminal offence under s. 34 (3). The Secretary of State has the power to make regulations concerning the procedure for or in connection with references to advisory committees and the making of reports to the Minister. The statutory instrument containing the draft regulations will be subject to the negative resolution procedure. Further details on the conduct and constitution of the advisory committee are found in Sch. 6. To date, no regulations have been made. [**265**]

It is hoped that these regulations might throw some light on how a trade union is expected to deploy an argument on a general level, that certain information should be imparted to it when it will not be given the substance of the information itself. It will not always be obvious from the nature of the information why special reasons preclude its dissemination. If this is not so, then it might have been wiser to elaborate more fully in the Act what constitutes "special reasons". Apart from the "special reason" described in s. 31 (4) (a), which will vary from case to case, the other reasons might reasonably be held to apply, in respect of the limited number of items enumerated in s. 30 (2) (a)–(k), to all enterprises which satisfy the narrow criteria needed to satisfy the definition of "relevant undertaking" in s. 28 (2). [**266**]

CONFIDENTIALITY AND OFFENCES

Information provided to the Minister and which has not been furnished to trade unions is confidential. No person may disclose information provided to him under the procedures in Part IV of the Act without the consent of the person providing the information, except: to a Government department (including a Northern Ireland department) for the purpose of the exercise of its functions, to a committee constituted to hear a reference under s. 32 and to any expert that committee may call upon to assist it, and to the Manpower Services Commission, the Employment Services Agency or the Training Services Agency. These latter bodies were established under the Employment and Training Act 1973 (A.L.S. Vol. 221), and although they perform functions which are comparable to those discharged by Government departments, they are not legally so defined (s. 33 (1)). It should be noted that information *cannot* be passed to the National Enterprise Board *without* the company's consent. These prohibitions apply both to the civil servants in Government departments and the agencies mentioned above, as well as to the members and staff of the advisory committees. It is arguable that such a confidentiality provision is otiose and that s. 2 of the Official Secrets Act 1911 would be equally effective, though its inclusion makes the point entirely clear and perhaps provides reassurance. **[267]**

Information may also be divulged without the consent of the company or companies concerned when it is sought for use in investigating the possible commission of an offence, or in connection with any criminal proceedings consequent on such an investigation, or in a report of any proceedings. This exception provides for disclosure in connection with *any* offence and not only those arising from the Act. **[268]**

There is no comparable provision requiring information provided by the company to trade unions to be treated by the trade union as confidential. Not only would such a provision be exceedingly difficult to enforce and place trade union officials in difficult situations, particularly in relation to any fiduciary duties they may owe, but it would also be undesirable to prevent trade union officials from discussing the information so obtained with their members. The *rationale* of this part of the Act rests on the effectiveness of the screening procedure preventing sensitive information from passing to the trade unions. By passing information to the trade unions the company may itself be placed in a difficult situation: chapter 2 of the listing agreement that all publicly quoted companies must enter into with the Stock Exchange states as follows, "Directors should not divulge price sensitive information in such a way as to place in a privileged position any person or class or category of persons outside the company and its advisers". It is a reasonable assumption that most though not all "relevant undertakings" will be publicly quoted companies. Equality of information is judged essential in order to ensure an orderly market in the securities of the company. The surest way any company can avoid being in breach of its listing agreement would be for it to pass the information given to the trade union to its shareholders: there is nothing in the Act placing a constraint on this course of action. **[269]**

The offences which are judged necessary to enforce the information disclosure provisions of the Act are set out in s. 34. Under s. 34 (1) it is an offence to refuse or to fail without reasonable excuse to comply with a requirement of a preliminary notice issued under s. 28. It is also an offence to refuse or fail without reasonable cause to furnish information required under Part IV of the Act. The provisions are self-explanatory and mirror a similar provision in the

Statistics of Trade Act 1947, s. 10 (3). The offences are not of strict liability and if a reasonable excuse is shown, for example, that the information is not available at all or in the form required no offence will be committed. If, in furnishing such information, a person makes a statement which he knows to be false in a material particular or recklessly makes a statement which is false in a material particular, this will constitute an offence. The clear purpose of this provision is to prevent a person avoiding his duties by providing information which is either knowingly wrong or which has been insufficiently considered. The offence will extend to forecasts, since a forecast can be false in the sense that it is not a genuine forecast; it may also be made recklessly. The offence is not to prophesy but to prophesy recklessly. A limitation period exists in respect of false and reckless statements: summary proceedings must be brought within three years of the commission of the offence and within six months from the date on which evidence sufficient in the opinion of the prosecutor, attested by his certificate to this effect, to warrant the proceedings came to his knowledge. The offences described above are each punishable, on summary conviction, by a fine not exceeding £400. If after conviction a person persists in refusing to furnish the required information, without reasonable cause, a further offence is committed and the person will be liable on summary conviction to a fine not exceeding £40 for each day on which the default is continued. For the continuing fine to be levied it will be necessary for the offender to have been convicted on two occasions, first for the original default, and second, for the continuing default. [**270**]

Proceedings for the offences described above require the consent of the Attorney-General in England and Wales or of the Attorney-General for Northern Ireland before they can be instituted. Without such a provision any person can prosecute in England, Wales and Northern Ireland. In Scotland, all prosecutions are brought by the Procurator fiscal. This provision ensures an element of political control over the prosecutions of offences (s. 34 (8)). [**271**]

It is an offence for a person to disclose information contrary to s. 33. The penalties for committing the offence are, on summary conviction, a fine not exceeding £200 or a prison sentence of three months or both; and, on conviction on indictment, imprisonment for a term not exceeding two years or to a fine, or both (s. 34 (3)). [**272**]

Where an offence is committed by a body corporate and is proved to have been committed with the consent or connivance or through the neglect of an officer of the company, or by someone purporting to hold such office, the individual as well as the body corporate may be guilty of the offence and punished accordingly (s. 34 (6)). This is a common enough provision which deals with the case of an offence committed by a body corporate or other legal person, i.e. a Scottish firm, which is managed by separate natural persons. Thus, the affairs of a company are managed by its directors and they will be the persons at whose instigation the offence was committed. The reference to a Scottish firm is necessary because such a firm is not a body corporate: it is a legal person distinct from the partners who compose it, but does not have corporate status. [**273**]

When a body corporate is managed by its members, a member shall be treated for the purposes of s. 34 (6) as if he were a director of the body corporate.

Again, this is a common form provision relevant to the responsibilities of the members of the boards of nationalised industries (s. 34 (7)). The jurisdiction of the summary courts is delimited by s. 34 (8), so that proceedings for offences under the Act may be taken against a body corporate where that body corporate has a place of business and against any other person wherever he may be, and not merely where the offence is committed, which would otherwise be the case. [**274**]

DISCLOSURE OF INFORMATION BY GOVERNMENT

The requirements contained in Sch. 5 constitute a significant change in the conduct of economic policy and represent a remarkable example of the influence that a backbench Member of Parliament can still bring to bear on a Government Bill even in the teeth of Government opposition. The White Paper stated, at para. 22, that ". . . The Government's projections and the companies' own intentions and plans will interact on each other: the primary purpose of a Planning Agreement is that they should. In producing their projections the Government will need to take account of companies' own plans, while the companies will for their part want to know the Government's views on the likely development of the economy . . . The question is not whether Government projections should be supplied . . . but which projections, given the unavoidable uncertainties, are likely to be of most value". On publication of the Bill, however, there was no mention of disclosure of information by Government. [**275**]

The primary purpose of Treasury forecasting was, and remains, to assist in the formulation of Government policy, not to assist and inform the private sector. Indeed, publication of Treasury short-term forecasts might have a deleterious or counter-productive effect, with companies anticipating Government policy changes. In short, there is a perceived danger that the Treasury's sophisticated prophesying would become self-fulfilling. [**276**]

Under Dr. Bray's amendment, which was subsequently redrafted by the Government, a *duty* is placed on the Treasury to maintain a computerised "macro-economic model" suitable for demonstrating the likely effects on economic events in the United Kingdom of different assumptions about the following matters, namely:

(a) Government economic policies;
(b) economic events outside the United Kingdom; and,
(c) such (if any) other matters as appear to the Treasury from time to time as likely to have a substantial effect on economic events in the United Kingdom. [**277**]

A "macro-economic model" is a system of mathematical relationships representing the more important economic inter-relationships in the economy as a whole, with the addition of certain exogenous variables, such as import prices. The Treasury model should enable quarterly forecasts to be made on any of the following matters:

(i) the level of gross domestic product;
(ii) unemployment;
(iii) the balance of payments on current account;

(iv) the general index of retail prices;
(v) average earnings; and
(vi) any other economic variables as are appropriate in the opinion of the Treasury from time to time.   [**278**]

The first major innovation is contained in Sch. 5, para. 5. This Treasury model will be available for use by the public to make forecasts based upon their own assumptions. In this way, the model which, according to Dr. Bray, has suffered from ". . . isolation, inaccessibility and inadequate testing and development" will be exposed to critical scrutiny. A reasonable fee will be levied for this privilege. It should be noted that Dr. Bray's original formulation permitted access to other Government departments, which it is understood they did not have, and presumably still do not.   [**279**]

The second innovation consists of the requirement that the Treasury must publish half-yearly forecasts, produced with the aid of the model ". . . on such matters and based on such alternative assumptions as appear to them to be appropriate". Once again, the rigour of Dr. Bray's formulation has been tempered by expediency: there is no requirement on the Treasury to publish forecasts of the items (i)–(vi) above. It is for the Treasury to decide which forecasts would be appropriate for them to publish. It was suggested that forecasts for example, relating to wage rates, the level of prices or the behaviour of exchange rates might in certain circumstances be prejudicial to the national interest. Any published forecast must, wherever possible, indicate the margin of error attached to it and the Treasury must occasionally publish an analysis of the errors of such forecasts which can be attributable to the structure of the model itself, rather than to the unrealistic choice of assumptions adopted.
[**280**]

As a postscript, if a Minister proposes to enter or has entered into a Planning Agreement with a body corporate, he is under a duty to accede to the undertaking's request to demonstrate the relationship between the undertaking and the national economy. An example of this liason might consist of the Government sharing its assumptions about the effect on sales of the undertaking's products following changes in taxation or of the exchange rate.   [**281**]

The Schedule has the effect of building, in an imaginative way, a bridge between national economic policy and industrial policy.   [**282**]

THE INDUSTRY ACT 1975
(1975 c. 68)

ARRANGEMENT OF SECTIONS
PART I
NATIONAL ENTERPRISE BOARD
Establishment of Board

PART II
POWERS IN RELATION TO TRANSFERS OF CONTROL OF IMPORTANT MANUFACTURING UNDERTAKINGS TO NON-RESIDENTS

PART III
PLANNING AGREEMENTS ETC.
Planning agreements

Selective financial assistance

Shipbuilding

An Act to establish a National Enterprise Board; to confer on the Secretary of State power to prohibit the passing to persons not resident in the United Kingdom of control of undertakings engaged in manufacturing industry, and power to acquire compulsorily the capital or assets of such undertakings where control has passed to such persons or there is a probability that it will pass; to amend the Industry Act 1972 and the Development of Inventions Act 1967; to make provision for the disclosure of information relating to manufacturing undertakings to the Secretary of State or the Minister of Agriculture, Fisheries and Food, and to trade unions; and for connected purposes [12th November 1975]

PART I

NATIONAL ENTERPRISE BOARD

Establishment of Board

1. The National Enterprise Board

(1) There shall be a body to be called the National Enterprise Board (in this Act referred to as "the Board") having the functions specified in the following provisions of this Act.

(2) The Board shall consist of a chairman and not less than eight nor more than sixteen other members.

(3) The chairman and other members of the Board shall be appointed by the Secretary of State.

(4) The Secretary of State may appoint one or more of the Board's members to be deputy chairman or deputy chairmen.

(5) The Board, with the approval of the Secretary of State, may appoint a chief executive of the Board.

(6) It is hereby declared that the Board shall not be regarded as the servant or agent of the Crown, or as enjoying any status, immunity or privilege of the Crown, and that the Board's property is not to be regarded as the property of, or property held on behalf of, the Crown.

(7) The Board shall not be exempt, except as provided by paragraph 18 of Schedule 1 below, from any tax, duty, rate, levy or other charge whatsoever, whether general or local.

(8) The Secretary of State shall maintain a register of members' financial interests and shall ensure that all members of the Board enter statements of such of their financial interests as, were they Members of the House of Commons, they would be required to register in accordance with resolutions of that House any such resolution being construed, in its application to members of the Board, with appropriate modifications.

(9) Schedules 1 and 2 to this Act shall have effect. [283]

2. General purposes and functions

(1) The purposes for which the Board may exercise their functions are—

    (a) the development or assistance of the economy of the United Kingdom or any part of the United Kingdom;

    (b) the promotion in any part of the United Kingdom of industrial efficiency and international competitiveness; and

(c) the provision, maintenance or safeguarding of productive employment in any part of the United Kingdom.

(2) The functions of the Board shall be—

    (a) establishing, maintaining or developing, or promoting or assisting the establishment, maintenance or development of any industrial undertaking;

    (b) promoting or assisting the reorganisation or development of an industry or any undertaking in an industry;

    (c) extending public ownership into profitable areas of manufacturing industry;

    (d) promoting industrial democracy in undertakings which the Board control; and

    (e) taking over publicly owned securities and other publicly owned property, and holding and managing securities and property which are taken over.

(3) The Board may do anything, whether in the United Kingdom or elsewhere, which is calculated to facilitate the discharge of the functions specified in subsection (2) above or is incidental or conducive to their discharge.

(4) In particular, but not so as to derogate from the generality of subsection (3) above, the Board shall have power—

    (a) to acquire, hold and dispose of securities;

    (b) to form bodies corporate;

    (c) to form partnerships with other persons;

    (d) to make loans;

    (e) to guarantee obligations (arising out of loans or otherwise) incurred by other persons;

    (f) to acquire and dispose of land, premises, plant, machinery and equipment and other property;

    (g) to make land, premises, plant, machinery and equipment and other property available for use by other persons; and

    (h) to provide services in relation to finance, management, administration or organisation of industry.

(5) For the avoidance of doubt it is hereby declared that the foregoing provisions of this section relate only to the capacity of the Board as a statutory corporation, and nothing in the said provisions shall be construed as authorising the disregard by the Board of any enactment or rule of law. [284]

3. Exercise by Board of powers to give selective financial assistance under Industry Act 1972

(1) In any case where it appears to the Secretary of State that the powers conferred on him by section 7 or 8 of the Industry Act 1972 (powers to give selective financial assistance) are exercisable and ought to be exercised, the Secretary of State, with the consent of the Treasury, may direct the Board to exercise them; and the Board shall not require the consent of the Treasury to the exercise of any such powers in pursuance of such a direction.

(2) It shall be the Board's duty to give effect to any such direction.

(3) The Secretary of State shall consult the Board before giving any such direction.

(4) A direction may specify—

    (*a*) the purpose for which and manner in which the Board are to exercise the powers,

    (*b*) the amount of assistance that they are to give, and

    (*c*) terms and conditions on which the assistance is to be given.

(5) Nothing in a subsequent direction shall relieve the Board of a contractual liability to which they are subject in consequence of an earlier direction.

(6) As soon as practicable after the Secretary of State has given a direction under this section he shall lay before each House of Parliament a statement specifying—

    (*a*) the amount of assistance that the Board are to give in pursuance of the direction;

    (*b*) how and to whom they are to give it; and

    (*c*) where it is to be given under section 7 of the Industry Act 1972, the assisted area in which the undertaking for which it is provided is or will be situated.

(7) The Board's report for any accounting year shall specify any direction that has been given under this section during that year and give the information concerning it that is required to be specified in a statement under subsection (6) above.

(8) In any case where the Board are exercising the Secretary of State's powers in pursuance of a direction under this section, sections 7 (4) and 8 (3) (*a*) of the Industry Act 1972 (each of which requires the consent of a company to the acquisition of its shares or stock) shall be construed, notwithstanding the fact that the direction has been given, as requiring the Secretary of State (and not the Board) to obtain the consent.

(9) If the Board acquire property in pursuance of any such direction, the Secretary of State shall reimburse them the consideration given for the acquisition and the costs and expenses of and incidental to it.

(10) If they make a grant in pursuance of any such direction, he shall pay them a sum equal to the amount of the grant.

(11) If they make a loan in pursuance of any such direction, he shall make them a loan of the same amount and, subject to subsection (12) below, on such terms as he considers appropriate.

(12) The terms of a loan under subsection (11) above shall only require the Board to repay the loan when the debtor repays them the loan which they made him.

(13) If the Board give assistance in pursuance of any such direction by way of any form of insurance or guarantee, the Secretary of State shall assume a correlative liability towards them.

(14) Any reference in subsection (6) or (8) of section 8 of the Industry Act 1972 to sums paid or liabilities assumed by the Secretary of State under that section shall include a reference to sums paid or liabilities assumed by the Board in exercising, by virtue of this section, the powers conferred on the Secretary of State by that section.

(15) The sums to be deducted from the aggregate of the amounts mentioned in paragraphs (*a*) and (*b*) of section 8 (6) of the Industry Act 1972 shall include, in any case where by virtue of this section the Board exercise the powers conferred on the Secretary of State by that section, any sum received by the Secre-

tary of State from the Board by way of repayment of loans to them under subsection (11) above, or repayment of principal sums paid to meet a liability towards the Board assumed by the Secretary of State under subsection (13) above.

(16) The Secretary of State may pay any administrative expenses of the Board under this section.

(17) It is hereby declared that nothing in this section affects—

    (a) the power conferred on the Secretary of State by subsection (7) of section 8 of the Industry Act 1972 (power to increase the limit on financial assistance under that section), or

    (b) the duty imposed on him by subsection (8) of that section (duty to obtain a resolution of the House of Commons for assistance in excess of £5 million),

or confers or imposes any corresponding power or duty on the Board.

(18) For the avoidance of doubt it is hereby declared, without prejudice to the generality of section 1 (6) above, that powers exercised by the Board under this section are not exercised on behalf of the Crown or of any Government department. [**285**]

4. Overseas Aid

The Board may, with the consent of the Secretary of State, enter into and carry out agreements with the Minister of Overseas Development under which the Board act, at the expense of that Minister, as the instrument by means of which technical assistance is furnished by the Minister in exercise of the power conferred by section 1 (1) of the Overseas Aid Act 1966; and the Board may, with the consent of both the Secretary of State and the said Minister, enter into and carry out agreements under which the Board, for any purpose specified in the said section 1 (1), furnish technical assistance in a country or territory outside the United Kingdom against reimbursement to them of the cost of furnishing that assistance. [**286**]

5. Transfer of publicly owned property to Board

(1) Subject to subsection (2) below, nothing in this Act or in any other enactment (including, subject to any express provision to the contrary, an enactment contained in an Act passed after this Act) shall prevent the transfer to the Board or the Board's nominees of any publicly owned securities or other publicly owned property.

(2) Publicly owned securities and other publicly owned property may only be transferred to the Board or the Board's nominees with the consent of the Secretary of State or in accordance with any general authority given by the Secretary of State.

(3) The Secretary of State shall lay before each House of Parliament a copy of any general authority given by him under subsection (2) above.

(4) Subject to subsections (5) and (6) below, if—

    (a) the Secretary of State has given a consent under subsection (2) above; and

    (b) the consideration for the transfer has been determined; and

    (c) its amount exceeds £1 million,

the Secretary of State shall lay before each House of Parliament a statement specifying—

(i) the securities or other property to be transferred;
(ii) the transferor;
(iii) the consideration; and
(iv) the date of his consent.

(5) If the Secretary of State has given a consent under subsection (2) above before the amount of the consideration for the transfer has been determined, he shall lay before each House of Parliament, unless it appears to him to be unlikely that the amount of the consideration will exceed £1 million, a statement specifying the matters, other than the consideration, that are required to be specified in a statement under subsection (4) above.

(6) When a statement has been laid under subsection (5) above, the Secretary of State shall lay before each House of Parliament a statement specifying the consideration for the transfer as soon as practicable after its amount has been determined. [287]

6. Financial duties of Board

(1) It shall be the duty of the Secretary of State to determine the financial duties of the Board; and different determinations may be made in relation to different assets and activities of the Board.

(2) The Secretary of State shall not make a determination except with the approval of the Treasury and after consultation with the Board, and shall give the Board notice of every determination.

(3) It shall be the duty of the Secretary of State and the Treasury, before making a determination, to satisfy themselves that the duties to be imposed on the Board are likely, taken together, to result in an adequate return on capital employed by the Board.

(4) A determination—

(a) may relate to a period beginning before the date on which it is made and
(b) may contain incidental or supplemental provisions. [288]

7. General power of Secretary of State to give Board directions

(1) Subject to subsection (2) below, the Secretary of State may give the Board directions of a general or specific character as to the exercise of their functions; and it shall be the duty of the Board to give effect to any such directions.

(2) The Secretary of State shall consult the Board about any proposed direction under this section.

(3) Subject to paragraph 8 (4) of Schedule 2 below, when the Secretary of State gives a direction under this section, he shall either—

(a) lay a copy of the direction before each House of Parliament within 28 days of giving it; or
(b) lay a copy later, but lay with it a statement of the reason why a copy was not laid within 28 days.

(4) The Board's report for any accounting year shall set out any direction given under this section during that year. [288A]

Limits on Board's powers

8. Financial limits

(1) The aggregate amount outstanding, otherwise than by way of interest, in respect of—

   (a) the general external borrowing of the Board and their wholly owned subsidiaries;

     (b) sums issued by the Treasury in fulfilment of guarantees under paragraph 4 of Schedule 2 below and not repaid to the Treasury;

     (c) sums paid to the Board under paragraph 5 (1) of that Schedule;

     (d) loans guaranteed by the Board otherwise than under section 3 above;

shall not exceed the limit specified in subsection (2) below.

(2) The said limit shall be £700 million, but the Secretary of State may by order made with the consent of the Treasury raise the limit to not more than £1,000 million.

(3) Such an order shall not be made unless a draft of it has been approved by resolution of the House of Commons.

(4) In subsection (1) above "general external borrowing" means—

   (a) in relation to the Board, sums borrowed by them other than—

     (i) sums borrowed from a body corporate which is one of the Board's wholly owned subsidiaries at the time of the loan;

     (ii) any sums mentioned in subsection (1) (b) above; or

     (iii) sums borrowed by the Board for the purpose of giving assistance under section 3 above; and

     (b) in relation to a wholly owned subsidiary of the Board, sums borrowed by it when it was such a subsidiary other than sums borrowed from the Board or from another wholly owned subsidiary;

but does not include any debt assumed by the Board under paragraph 6 (1) of Schedule 2 below. [**289**]

9. The Board and the media

(1) Subject to subsection (2) below, neither the Board nor any of the Board's subsidiaries—

   (a) shall commence a business of publishing newspapers, magazines or other periodicals for sale to the public in the United Kingdom; or

   (b) enter into any contract with the Independent Broadcasting Authority for the provision of programmes.

(2) Subsection (1) above does not apply to periodicals wholly or mainly concerned with the activities of the Board or any of the Board's subsidiaries.

(3) Subject to subsection (4) below, neither the Board nor any of the Board's subsidiaries shall acquire any of the share capital of a body corporate if a substantial part of the undertaking—

   (a) of that body corporate, or

   (b) of a group of companies of which it is the holding company,

consists of carrying on—

     (i) a business such as is mentioned in paragraph (a) of subsection (1) above, or

     (ii) the activities of a programme contractor.

(4) Subsection (3) above shall not prevent the acquisition of share capital of a body corporate if the acquisition is made in pursuance of a direction under section 3 above.

(5) Subject to subsections (7) and (8) below, if the Board or any of the Board's subsidiaries acquire any of the share capital of a body corporate which carries on any such business as is mentioned in subsection (1) (*a*) above, it shall be their duty to exercise their voting power with a view to securing that the body corporate disposes of the business as soon as practicable.

(6) Subject to subsections (7) and (8) below, if the Board or any of the Board's subsidiaries acquire any of the share capital of a body corporate which has any interest, direct or indirect, in a body corporate which carries on such a business, it shall be their duty to exercise their voting power with a view to securing that the capital of the body corporate which carries on that business is disposed of as soon as practicable.

(7) The Secretary of State may direct that the Board or a subsidiary of the Board shall not be under any duty imposed by subsection (5) or (6) above during such time as the direction is in force.

(8) The Secretary of State may only give such a direction as is mentioned in subsection (7) above if he is of the opinion that without such a direction serious commercial injury would be caused to any newspaper, magazine or periodical concerned.

(9) If the Board or any of the Board's subsidiaries acquire any of the share capital of a body corporate which is a programme contractor, they shall consult the Independent Broadcasting Authority as to the steps that they are to take with regard to that share capital and obey any direction given by that Authority.

(10) Without prejudice to the foregoing provisions of this section, it shall be the duty of the Board and of any of the Board's subsidiaries to use any power to control or influence the carrying on of a business such as is mentioned in paragraph (*a*) of subsection (1) above or of the activities of a programme contractor only in relation to financial or commercial matters.

(11) In this section "programme contractor" has the meaning assigned to it by section 2 (3) of the Independent Broadcasting Authority Act 1973.

10. Other limits on Board's powers

(1) Neither the Board nor any of their subsidiaries shall acquire any of the share capital of a body corporate except with the consent of the Secretary of State or in accordance with any general authority given by the Secretary of State—

> (*a*) if its acquisition would entitle the Board to exercise or control the exercise of 30 per cent. or more of the votes at any general meeting of the body corporate; or
>
> (*b*) if the value of the consideration for its acquisition, together with the value of any consideration paid for share capital of that body corporate previously acquired, would exceed £10,000,000.

(2) Subsection (1) (*a*) above shall not restrict the acquisition of share capital of a body corporate which gives a right to vote exercisable only in restricted circumstances.

(3) Nothing in subsection (1) above shall be taken to restrict the power to form bodies corporate conferred on the Board by section 2 (4) (*b*) above.

(4) In any case where the Board hold share capital such as is mentioned in subsection (2) above, the fact that they hold it shall be disregarded for the purpose of determining whether subsection (1) (*a*) above prevents their acquisition of further share capital of the same body corporate. [**291**]

PART II

POWERS IN RELATION TO TRANSFERS OF CONTROL OF IMPORTANT MANUFACTURING UNDERTAKINGS TO NON-RESIDENTS

11. General extent of powers in relation to control of important manufacturing undertakings

(1) The powers conferred by this Part of this Act shall have effect in relation to changes of control of important manufacturing undertakings.

(2) In this Part of this Act—

"important manufacturing undertaking" means an undertaking which, in so far as it is carried on in the United Kingdom, is wholly or mainly engaged in manufacturing industry and appears to the Secretary of State to be of special importance to the United Kingdom or to any substantial part of the United Kingdom. [**292**]

12. Meaning of "change of control"

(1) There is a change of control of an important manufacturing undertaking for the purposes of this Part of this Act only upon the happening of a relevant event.

(2) In subsection (1) above "relevant event" means any event as a result of which—

(*a*) the person carrying on the whole or part of the undertaking ceases to be resident in the United Kingdom;

(*b*) a person not resident in the United Kingdom acquires the whole or part of the undertaking;

(*c*) a body corporate resident in the United Kingdom but controlled by a person not so resident acquires the whole or part of the undertaking;

(*d*) a person not resident in the United Kingdom becomes able to exercise or control the exercise of the first, second or third qualifying percentage of votes in a body corporate carrying on the whole or part of the undertaking or in any other body corporate which is in control of such a body; or

(*e*) a person resident in the United Kingdom and able to exercise or control the exercise of the first, second or third qualifying percentage of votes in a body corporate carrying on the whole or part of the undertaking or in any other body corporate which is in control of such a body ceases to be resident in the United Kingdom.

(3) For the purposes of subsection (2) above—

(*a*) a body corporate or individual entitled to cast 30 per cent. or more of the votes that may be cast at any general meeting of a body corporate, is in control of that body; and

(*b*) control of a body corporate which has control of another body corporate gives control of the latter body.

(4) Any power to direct the holder of shares or stock in a body corporate as to the exercise of his votes at a general meeting of that body corporate is to be treated as entitlement to cast the votes in respect of the shares or stock in question.

(5) Two or more persons acting together in concert may be treated as a single person for the purposes of any provision of this Part of this Act relating to change of control.

(6) For the purposes of this Part of this Act—

(*a*) the first qualifying percentage of votes is 30 per cent.;
(*b*) the second qualifying percentage is 40 per cent.; and
(*c*) the third qualifying percentage is 50 per cent.;

and the references to votes in this subsection are references to votes that may be cast at a general meeting. [**293**]

13. Power to make orders

(1) If it appears to the Secretary of State—

(*a*) that there is a serious and immediate probability of a change of control of an important manufacturing undertaking; and
(*b*) that that change of control would be contrary to the interests of the United Kingdom, or contrary to the interests of any substantial part of the United Kingdom,

he may by order (in this Part of this Act referred to as a "prohibition order") specify the undertaking and

(i) prohibit that change of control; and
(ii) prohibit or restrict the doing of things which in his opinion would constitute or lead to it;

and may make such incidental or supplementary provision in the order as appears to him to be necessary or expedient.

(2) Subject to subsection (3) below, if—

(*a*) the conditions specified in paragraphs (*a*) and (*b*) of subsection (1) above are satisfied, or
(*b*) a prohibition order has been made in relation to an important manufacturing undertaking, or
(*c*) the Secretary of State has learnt of circumstances which appear to him to constitute a change of control of an important manufacturing undertaking, occurring on or after 1st February 1975, and is satisfied that that change is contrary to the interests of the United Kingdom, or contrary to the interests of any substantial part of the United Kingdom,

the Secretary of State may by order made with the approval of the Treasury (in this Part of this Act referred to as a "vesting order") direct that on a day specified in the order—

(i) share capital and loan capital to which this subsection applies, or
(ii) any assets which are employed in the undertaking,

shall vest in the Board or in himself or in nominees for the Board or himself and may make such incidental or supplementary provision in the order as appears to him to be necessary or expedient.

(3) A vesting order may only be made if the Secretary of State is satisfied that the order is necessary in the national interest and that, having regard to

all the circumstances, that interest cannot, or cannot appropriately, be protected in any other way.

(4) The share capital and loan capital to which subsection (2) above applies are—

   (a) in any case where the Secretary of State considers that the interests mentioned in subsection (2) (c) above cannot, or cannot appropriately, be protected unless all the share capital of any relevant body corporate vests by virtue of the order, the share capital of that body corporate, together with so much (if any) of the loan capital of that body as may be specified in the order,

   (b) in any other case, that part of the share capital of any relevant body corporate which, at the time that the draft of the order is laid before Parliament under section 15 (3) below, appears to the Secretary of State to be involved in the change of control.

(5) In this section "relevant body corporate" means—

   (a) a body corporate incorporated in the United Kingdom carrying on in the United Kingdom as the whole or the major part of its business there the whole or part of an important manufacturing undertaking, or

   (b) a body corporate incorporated in the United Kingdom—

      (i) which is the holding company of a group of companies carrying on in the United Kingdom as the whole or the major part of their business there the whole or part of an important manufacturing undertaking, and

      (ii) as to which one of the conditions specified in subsection (6) below is satisfied.

(6) The conditions mentioned in subsection (5) above are—

   (a) that it appears to the Secretary of State that there is a serious and immediate probability of the happening of an event in relation to the company which would constitute a change of control of the undertaking, or

   (b) that the Secretary of State has learnt of circumstances relating to the company which appear to him to constitute a change of control of the undertaking on or after 1st February 1975. [**294**]

14. Notices to extend vesting orders to other holdings

(1) Where 30 per cent. or more of the share capital of the body corporate vests in the Secretary of State or the Board by virtue of a vesting order, the Secretary of State shall serve on the holders of all the share capital that does not so vest, and on any other persons who to his knowledge have a present or prospective right to subscribe for share capital of the body corporate, within 28 days of the making of the order, a notice informing them of the making of the order and of the right of each of them to require the order to extend to the share capital or rights held by him.

(2) The recipient of a notice under subsection (1) above may, within three months of the date of the notice, serve on the Secretary of State a counter-notice requiring the order to extend to the share capital or rights held by the recipient in the body corporate.

(3) A vesting order shall have effect, from the date of a counter-notice, as if the share capital or rights specified in the notice had been specified in the vesting order.

(4) Subsections (1) to (3) above shall have the same effect in relation to share capital vesting in nominees for the Secretary of State or the Board as in relation to share capital vesting as mentioned in those subsections. [295]

15. Parliamentary control of orders

(1) A prohibition order shall be laid before Parliament after being made, and the order shall cease to have effect at the end of the period of 28 days beginning on the day on which it was made (but without prejudice to anything previously done by virtue of the order or to the making of a new order) unless during that period it is approved by resolution of each House of Parliament.

(2) In reckoning the period mentioned in subsection (1) above no account shall be taken of any time during which Parliament is dissolved or prorogued or during which both Houses are adjourned for more than four days.

(3) A vesting order shall not be made unless a draft of the order has been laid before and approved by resolution of each House of Parliament.

(4) A draft of a vesting order shall not be laid before Parliament—

(a) in a case such as is mentioned in paragraph (a) of section 13 (2) above, after the end of a period of three months from the service of a notice under section 16 (7) below of the Secretary of State's intention to lay the draft before Parliament;

(b) in a case such as is mentioned in paragraph (b) of that subsection (2), after the end of a period of three months from the making of the prohibition order unless such circumstances as are mentioned in paragraph (a) or (c) of that subsection exist at the time when the draft of the order is laid before Parliament under subsection (3) above; and

(c) in a case such as is mentioned in paragraph (c) of that subsection, after the end of a period of three months from the date on which the Secretary of State learnt of circumstances such as are mentioned in that paragraph.

(5) On the expiry of 28 days from the laying of the draft of a vesting order in a House of Parliament the order shall proceed in that House, whether or not it has been referred to a Committee under Standing Orders of that House relating to Private Bills, as if its provisions would require to be enacted by a Public Bill which cannot be referred to such a Committee.

(6) In reckoning, for purposes of proceedings in either House of Parliament, the period mentioned in subsection (5) above, no account shall be taken of any time during which Parliament is dissolved or prorogued or during which that House is adjourned for more than four days. [296]

16. Contents of vesting order

(1) Without prejudice to the generality of section 13 (2) above, a vesting order may contain provisions by virtue of which rights, liabilities or incumbrances to which assets or capital which will vest by virtue of the order are subject—

(a) will be extinguished in consideration of the payment of compensation as provided under section 19 below, or

(b) will be transferred to the Secretary of State or the Board, or

(c) will be charged on the compensation under section 19 below.

(2) A vesting order which provides for the vesting of assets employed in an undertaking may prohibit or set aside any transfer of assets so employed or of any right in respect of such assets.

(3) A vesting order may include such provisions as the Secretary of State considers necessary or expedient to safeguard—

  (a) any capital which will vest by virtue of the order; and
  (b) any assets—
    (i) of a body corporate whose capital will so vest, or
    (ii) of any subsidiary of such a body corporate;

and may in particular, but without prejudice to the generality of this subsection, prohibit or set aside the transfer of any such capital or assets or any right in respect of such capital or assets.

(4) A vesting order setting aside a transfer of capital or a transfer of assets such as are mentioned in subsection (2) above shall entitle the Secretary of State or the Board to recover the capital or assets transferred.

(5) A vesting order setting aside a transfer of assets such as are mentioned in subsection (3) (b) above shall entitle the body corporate or subsidiary to recover the assets transferred.

(6) Any vesting order setting aside a transfer shall give the person entitled to recover the capital or assets a right to be compensated in respect of the transfer.

(7) The transfers to which this section applies include transfers made before the draft of the order is laid before Parliament but after the Secretary of State has served notice on the person concerned of his intention to lay a draft order.

(8) In subsection (7) above "the person concerned" means—

  (a) in the case of an order such as is mentioned in paragraph (i) of section 13 (2) above, the relevant body corporate, and
  (b) in the case of an order such as is mentioned in paragraph (ii) of that subsection, the person carrying on the undertaking.

(9) The Secretary of State shall publish a copy of any such notice in the London Gazette, the Edinburgh Gazette and the Belfast Gazette as soon as practicable after he has served it. [**297**]

17. Remedies for contravention of prohibition orders

(1) No criminal proceedings shall lie against any person on the ground that he has committed, or aided, abetted, counselled or procured the commission of, or conspired or attempted to commit, or incited others to commit, any contravention of a prohibition order.

(2) Nothing in subsection (1) above shall limit any right of any person to bring civil proceedings in respect of any contravention or apprehended contravention of a prohibition order, and (without prejudice to the generality of the preceding words) compliance with any such order shall be enforceable by civil proceedings by the Crown for an injunction or interdict or for any other appropriate relief. [**298**]

18. Territorial scope of orders

(1) Nothing in a prohibition order shall have effect so as to apply to any person in relation to his conduct outside the United Kingdom unless he is—

  (a) a citizen of the United Kingdom and Colonies or,
  (b) a body corporate incorporated in the United Kingdom or,
  (c) a person carrying on business in the United Kingdom either alone or in partnership with one or more other persons,

but in a case falling within paragraph (*a*), (*b*) or (*c*) above, any such order may extend to acts or omissions outside the United Kingdom.

(2) For the purposes of this Part of this Act a body corporate shall be deemed not to be resident in the United Kingdom if it is not incorporated in the United Kingdom. [**299**]

19. Compensation orders

(1) No vesting order shall be made until there has also been laid before both Houses of Parliament an order (in this Part of this Act referred to as a "compensation order") providing for the payment of compensation for the acquisition of the capital or assets and for any extinguishment or transfer of rights, liabilities or encumbrances in question.

(2) A compensation order shall be subject to special parliamentary procedure.

(3) A compensation order—

(*a*) shall identify the persons or descriptions of persons to be paid compensation and determine their rights and duties in relation to any compensation paid to them;

(*b*) shall specify the manner in which compensation is to be paid;

(*c*) shall provide for the payment of interest on compensation in respect of the relevant period;

(*d*) may make different provision in relation to different descriptions of capital or assets and different rights, liabilities or incumbrances; and

(*e*) may contain incidental and supplementary provisions;

and in paragraph (*c*) above "the relevant period" means—

(i) in relation to capital or assets, the period commencing with the date on which the capital or assets vest in the Board or the Secretary of State or their or his nominees and ending with the date of payment of compensation; and

(ii) in relation to rights, liabilities and incumbrances, the period commencing with the date on which they are extinguished and ending on the date of payment.

(4) Compensation may be paid out—

(*a*) out of moneys provided by Parliament, or

(*b*) by the issue of government stock (that is to say, stock the principal whereof and the interest whereon is charged on the National Loans Fund with recourse to the Consolidated Fund),

and the power conferred by subsection (3) (*b*) above is a power to provide for compensation by one or both of the means specified in this subsection.

(5) The proviso to section 6 (2) of the Statutory Orders (Special Procedure) Act 1945 (power to withdraw an order or submit it to Parliament for further consideration by means of a Bill for its confirmation) shall have effect in relation to compensation orders as if for the words "may by notice given in the prescribed manner, withdraw the order or may" there were substituted the word "shall". [**300**]

20. Arbitration of disputes relating to vesting and compensation orders

(1) Any dispute to which this section applies shall be determined under Schedule 3 to this Act.

(2) Where any such dispute has been submitted to a tribunal constituted under that Schedule, any other dispute to which this section applies shall be determined by the same tribunal.

(3) This section applies to a dispute which arises out of a vesting order or a compensation order and to which one of the parties is the Secretary of State, the Board or a body corporate the whole or part of whose share capital has vested by virtue of the order in either of them or in nominees for either of them—

(a) if the provisions of the order require it to be submitted to arbitration; or

(b) if one of the parties wishes to be so submitted;

and where this section applies to a dispute which arises out of an order, it also applies to any dispute which arises out of a related order.

(4) A vesting order and a compensation order are related for the purposes of this section if they relate to the same capital or assets. [**301**]

Part III

Planning Agreements Etc.

Planning agreements

21. Financial assistance under Industry Act 1972 for bodies corporate which make planning agreements

(1) When a body corporate has made a planning agreement—

(a) the amount of grant under Part I of the Industry Act 1972 (regional development grant) in respect of approved capital expenditure incurred during the period mentioned in subsection (2) below in respect of any project identified in the agreement may be not less than—

(i) the percentage which is the prescribed percentage at the date of the planning agreement, or

(ii) in the case of a project which was also identified in a previous planning agreement, the percentage which was the prescribed percentage at the date of that agreement, and

(b) financial assistance in respect of any such project may be given under Part II of that Act,

without regard to any order under that Act or the Local Employment Act 1972 made after the date of the planning agreement by virtue of which, as the case may be, the grant or part of it could for any reason not have been paid or the financial assistance or part of it could not have been given.

(2) In this Act "planning agreement" means a voluntary arrangement as to the strategic plans of a body corporate for the future development in the United Kingdom over a specified period of an undertaking of the body corporate or of one or more of that body's subsidiaries, or a joint undertaking of the body corporate and one or more of its subsidiaries, being an arrangement entered into by the body corporate and any Minister of the Crown which in the opinion of that Minister is likely over the specified period to contribute significantly to national needs and objectives.

(3) When a body corporate makes a planning agreement, the Secretary of State shall lay a statement that the body corporate has made such an agreement before each House of Parliament. [302]

Selective financial assistance

22. Extension of powers to give selective financial assistance under Industry Act 1972

The provisions of Part I of Schedule 4 to this Act shall be made to the Industry Act 1972 and accordingly Part II of that Act shall have effect as set out in Part II of the Schedule. [303]

Shipbuilding

23. Increase in limits on credits

In subsection (3) of section 10 of the Industry Act 1972 (construction credits for ships and offshore installations) for "£1,400 million" there shall be substituted "£1,800 million". [304]

24. Renewal of guarantees

(1) In subsections (2) and (6) of that section, after the words "subsection (1)" there shall be inserted the words "or (7A)".

(2) After subsection (7) there shall be inserted the following subsections—

"(7A) The Secretary of State, with the consent of the Treasury, may renew—

(a) any guarantee given under section 7 of the Shipbuilding Industry Act 1967, and

(b) any guarantee given under this section, including a guarantee previously renewed by virtue of this subsection,

on the transfer of any liability to which it relates, or of part of any such liability, from a body corporate such as is mentioned in subsection (1) above to another such body corporate in the same group.

(7B) Two bodies corporate are in the same group for the purposes of subsection (7A) above if one is the other's holding company or both are subsidiaries of a third body corporate.".

(3) At the end of subsection (9) there shall be added the words "and 'holding company' and 'subsidiary' have the meanings assigned to them for the purposes of the Companies Act 1948 by section 154 of that Act, or for the purposes of the Companies Act (Northern Ireland) 1960 by section 148 of that Act.". [305]

25. Grants to supplement interest

After the said section 10 there shall be inserted the following section—

"10A. Interest grants

The Secretary of State, with the consent of the Treasury, may make a grant, on such terms and conditions as he may determine, to any person who is or has been a creditor in respect of principal money the payment of which has been guaranteed under section 10 above or section 7 of the

Shipbuilding Industry Act 1967, for the purpose of supplementing the interest receivable or received by him on that principal money (including interest for periods before the coming into force of this Act).". [**306**]

Amendment of Development of Inventions Act 1967

26. Relaxation of requirements as to approval of activities of the National Research Development Corporation

In section 4 (2) (*b*) of the Development of Inventions Act 1967 (Ministerial approval for activities of the National Research Development Corporation) for the words "£1,000" there shall be substituted the words "£20,000 or such other figure as the Secretary of State may by order made by statutory instrument with the approval of the Treasury direct"; and after that paragraph there shall be added (but not as part of it) the words "and any statutory instrument made by virtue of this subsection shall be subject to annulment in pursuance of a resolution of either House of Parliament". [**307**]

PART IV

DISCLOSURE OF INFORMATION

Disclosure by Government

27. Disclosure of information by Government

Ministers of the Crown and the Treasury shall publish, make available and provide access to information and analysis as specified in Schedule 5 to this Act.
[**308**]

Disclosure by Companies

28. Persons to whom duty to disclose information applies

(1) For the purpose of obtaining information which in the opinion of either of the Ministers is needed to form or to further national economic policies, or needed for consultations between Government, employers or workers on the outlook for a particular sector of manufacturing industry, including the outlook for the major companies in that sector, that Minister, if it appears to him that one of the following conditions is satisfied, namely—

    (*a*) that a company is carrying on in the United Kingdom an undertaking wholly or mainly engaged in manufacturing industry;

    (*b*) that a group of companies is carrying on in the United Kingdom an undertaking wholly or mainly engaged in manufacturing industry,

and if it also appears to him—

    (i) that the undertaking makes a significant contribution to a sector of such industry important to the economy of the United Kingdom or to that of any substantial part of the United Kingdom, and

    (ii) that it is desirable, for the purpose of obtaining information of that description, that the company or companies concerned should provide the Government and a representative of each relevant trade union with any such information relating to the undertaking,

may serve a preliminary notice on the company or companies concerned.

(2) In this Part of this Act—

"company or companies concerned" means—

(a) where it appears to the Minister that the condition mentioned in subsection (1) (a) above is satisfied, the company carrying on the undertaking, and

(b) where it appears to the Minister that the condition specified in subsection (1) (b) above is satisfied—

(i) the group's holding company, if that company is registered in the United Kingdom, and

(ii) all the companies in the group, if the holding company is not registered in the United Kingdom;

"preliminary notice" means a notice—

(a) stating which of the conditions specified in paragraphs (a) and (b) of subsection (1) above appears to the Minister to be satisfied in relation to the undertaking;

(b) informing the company or companies concerned that if the Minister is not satisfied that such information relating to the undertaking as is specified in paragraph (ii) of that subsection will be given voluntarily both to him and to a representative of each relevant trade union he will consider making an order under this section; and

(c) requiring them—

(i) to give a representative of each relevant trade union a notice of the service of the preliminary notice within 14 days of the date on which it is served; and

(ii) to give the Minister, within such reasonable time as may be specified in the preliminary notice, a list of representatives of relevant trade unions to whom they have given the notice mentioned in paragraph (i) above;

"relevant trade union" means an independent trade union, as defined in section 30 (1) of the Trade Union and Labour Relations Act 1974, which the company or companies concerned recognise for the purpose of negotiations about one or more of the matters specified in section 29 (1) of that Act in relation to persons employed in the relevant undertaking, or as to which the Advisory Conciliation and Arbitration Service has made a recommendation for such recognition under the Employment Protection Act 1975 which is operative within the meaning of section 15 of that Act; and

"relevant undertaking" means an undertaking in relation to which a preliminary notice states that a condition mentioned in paragraph (a) or (b) of subsection (1) above appears to the Minister to be satisfied.

(3) When a Minister serves a preliminary notice, he shall lay before each House of Parliament a statement that he has served it, specifying the company or companies concerned, the relevant undertaking and the date on which the notice was served.

(4) Subject to subsections (5) to (7) below, when a Minister has served a preliminary notice, he may by order declare that this Part of this Act applies to the company or companies concerned in respect of the relevant undertaking.

(5) A Minister shall not make an order under this section before the end of a period of 3 months from the service of the preliminary notice.

97

(6) A Minister shall not make such an order unless it appears to him that the company or companies concerned will not voluntarily furnish the information to him and to a representative of each relevant trade union.

(7) Before making an order a Minister shall give the company or companies concerned and the authorised representative of each relevant trade union an opportunity to make representations to him concerning it.

(8) An order shall be subject to annulment in pursuance of a resolution of either House of Parliament.

(9) The question what is a sector of an industry shall be determined by the Minister serving the preliminary notice. [**309**]

29. Meaning of "representative" and "authorised representative"

(1) In this Part of this Act—

> "authorised representative" means a representative of a relevant trade union to whom the company or companies concerned give—
>> (a) a notice of service of a preliminary notice, or
>> (b) a notice under subsection (2) below; and

> "representative" means an official or other person who is authorised by a relevant trade union to carry on negotiations about one or more of the matters specified in section 29 (1) of the Trade Union and Labour Relations Act 1974.

(2) If an authorised representative—

> (a) ceases to be a representative of the relevant trade union of which he is the authorised representative, or
> (b) gives the company or companies concerned notice that he desires to be discharged from acting as authorised representative of that union, or
> (c) ceases for any other reason to be available to act as that union's authorised representative,

it shall be the duty of the company or companies concerned—

> (i) to give another representative of the relevant trade union notice that he is to be the authorised representative of that union, and
> (ii) to give the Minister a notice requesting him to insert the name of the new representative in the list of authorised representatives in place of that of the old representative. [**310**]

30. Duty to give information to Minister

(1) A Minister who has made an order under section 28 above may by notice require the company or companies concerned to furnish him, in such manner and within such reasonable time as may be specified in the notice, and in such form as may be so specified, with such information as may be so specified relating to the business in the United Kingdom of the relevant undertaking, but not as to any matter except those specified in subsection (2) below.

(2) The matters mentioned in subsection (1) above are—

> (a) the persons employed in the undertaking, or persons normally so employed (but not specifically as to individuals);
> (b) the undertaking's capital expenditure;
> (c) fixed capital assets used in the undertaking;
> (d) any disposal or intended disposal of such assets;
> (e) any acquisition or intended acquisition of fixed capital assets for use in the undertaking;

(*f*) the productive capacity and capacity utilisation of the undertaking;
(*g*) the undertaking's output and productivity;
(*h*) sales of the undertaking's products;
(*i*) exports of those products by the undertaking;
(*j*) sales of industrial or intellectual property owned or used in connection with the undertaking, grants of rights in respect of such property, and contracts for any such sales or grants; and
(*k*) expenditure on any research or development programme.

(3) A notice may require information as to any of those matters—

(*a*) in relation to a specified date not earlier than the commencement of the most recently completed financial year of the person specified in the notice;
(*b*) in relation to a period commencing not earlier than the commencement of that year;
(*c*) in relation to a future specified date or a future specified period;

but a requirement which is made wholly or partly, in relation to a future specified date or a future specified period, is to be construed, to the extent that it relates to that date or that period, as a requirement only to give a forecast.

(4) The Minister shall send a copy of a notice under this section to the authorised representative of each relevant trade union.

(5) Nothing in this section shall be construed as enabling a Minister to require information about the details of know-how or of any research or development programme.

(6) In this section—

"industrial or intellectual property" includes, without prejudice to its generality, patents, designs, trade marks, know-how and copyrights, and

"know-how" has the meaning assigned to it by section 386 (7) of the Income and Corporation Taxes Act 1970. [**311**]

31. Information for trade unions

(1) Subject to subsections (2) to (8) below, after a Minister has received the information specified in a notice under section 30 above the Minister may serve—

(*a*) a further notice on the company or companies concerned provisionally requiring them to furnish to the authorised representative of each relevant trade union the whole or part of the information furnished to him under section 30 above, and
(*b*) a notice as to the furnishing of that information on each such representative,

and any notice served under this subsection shall specify a reasonable period, which shall not be less than 28 days, as the period within which references may be required under section 32 (1) below.

(2) A Minister shall not require information to be furnished if he considers that reasons of national policy or special reasons apply.

(3) For the purposes of this Act reasons of national policy apply if the Minister considers—

(*a*) that to furnish the information would be undesirable in the national interest; or (*b*) that the company or companies concerned could not furnish it without contravening a prohibition imposed by or under an enactment.

(4) For the purposes of this Act special reasons apply if the Minister considers—

(*a*) that the information was communicated to the company or companies concerned in confidence, or was information which they otherwise obtained in consequence of the confidence reposed in them by another person; or

(*b*) that the disclosure of the information would cause substantial injury to the undertaking; or

(*c*) that its disclosure would cause substantial injury to a substantial number of employees of the undertaking.

(5) A Minister shall not serve a notice under subsection (1) above without giving—

(*a*) to the company or companies concerned, and

(*b*) to the authorised representative of each relevant trade union,

an opportunity of making representations to him.

(6) The notice to be given to the company or companies concerned under subsection (1) above is a notice stating what information (if any) the Minister proposes to require them to furnish.

(7) The notice to be given to the authorised representatives under subsection (1) above is a notice stating whether or not the Minister proposes to require the company or companies concerned to furnish all the information furnished to him by them.

(8) If a notice given to authorised representatives under subsection (1) above states that the Minister does not propose to require the company or companies concerned to furnish all the information, it shall give such indication of the nature (without disclosing the substance) of any information which the Minister proposes should not be furnished for special reasons as will enable the representatives to consider whether or not they ought to exercise their right to require a reference under section 32 below. [**312**]

32. Release from duty to disclose information to trade union

(1) A Minister who has served a notice under section 31 above may by notice served within the period specified in that notice be required to make a reference to an advisory committee.

(2) Such a reference may be required—

(*a*) by the company or companies concerned, where the Minister proposes to require them to furnish information under section 31 above and they claim that the Minister's final decision ought to be that it should not be furnished because special reasons apply, or

(*b*) by the authorised representative of any relevant trade union, where the Minister proposes that some or all of the information furnished to him shall not be furnished to authorised representatives because special reasons apply.

(3) A Minister may himself refer to an advisory committee any proposal that some or all of the information furnished to him shall not be furnished to authorised representatives of relevant trade unions because special reasons apply.

(4) Schedule 6 to this Act shall have effect.

(5) The committee shall give the company or companies concerned and each relevant trade union's authorised representative an opportunity of making representations in relation to the matters to which the reference relates.

(6) The advisory committee shall make a report to the Minister after the close of their consideration of the reference, giving their findings of fact and their recommendations, and after considering any representations made under subsection (5) above.

(7) Where a matter has been referred to the committee, the Minister may make a final decision relating to his proposal only after receiving and considering the committee's report on it.

(8) Subject to subsection (13) below, where there has been a reference, the Minister shall notify—

(a) the company or companies concerned;
(b) the authorised representative of each relevant trade union; and
(c) the advisory committee,

of his final decision; and a notice under this subsection shall be treated as requiring the information specified in it to be furnished to each such representative within such reasonable time as may be so specified.

(9) The Minister's notice under subsection (8) above to the company or companies concerned and to the authorised representatives shall state whether or not he accepted the committee's advice.

(10) Where there has been no reference to the advisory committee or a reference has been withdrawn, the Minister may notify the company or companies concerned and each relevant trade union's authorised representative that his provisional notice under section 31 above is to be treated as containing his final decision.

(11) A notice under subsection (10) above shall state that the provisional notice is to be treated as requiring the information specified in it to be furnished to the authorised representative of each trade union within such reasonable time as may be specified in the notice under subsection (10) above.

(12) No such notice shall be given before the end of the period specified in the provisional notice.

(13) If—

(a) the Minister's final decision in relation to any information is that it shall be furnished to the representative of each relevant trade union, and
(b) in making that decision he rejected the committee's advice,

he shall make an order specifying the nature (without disclosing the substance) of the information to be furnished contrary to that advice, and accordingly requiring the company or companies concerned to furnish it to the representative of each relevant trade union within such reasonable time as may be specified in the order.

(14) An order under subsection (13) above shall be laid before Parliament after being made.

(15) An order under subsection (13) above shall not take effect if before the end of a period of 28 days from the date on which it is laid before Parliament either House resolves that an Address be presented to Her Majesty praying that it be annulled.

(16) If no such resolution is passed by either House, the order shall come into effect at the end of the said period.

(17) If such a resolution is passed by either House, Her Majesty may by Order in Council revoke the order.

(18) In reckoning the period of 28 days no account shall be taken of any time during which Parliament is dissolved or prorogued or during which both Houses are adjourned for more than 4 days.

(19) This section shall apply with appropriate modifications in any case where only part of the information furnished to the Minister falls to be disclosed to representatives of relevant trade unions.   [**313**]

33. Confidentiality

(1) Information to which this section applies shall not be disclosed without the consent of the person furnishing it except—

    (*a*) to a government department for the purposes of the exercise by that department of any of their functions;

    (*b*) for the purposes of a reference under section 32 above, to the advisory committee or to a person whose aid is called in under paragraph 5 of Schedule 6 to this Act;

    (*c*) to the Manpower Services Commission, the Employment Services Agency or the Training Services Agency established under the Employment and Training Act 1973; or

    (*d*) for use—

        (i) in investigating the possible commission of an offence,

        (ii) in connection with any criminal proceedings consequent on such an investigation, or

        (iii) in a report of any such proceedings.

(2) Subject to subsection (3) below, this section applies to information which has been furnished to a Minister under section 30 above but has not been furnished to authorised representatives under section 32 above.

(3) This section does not apply to any information at a time after a person has been convicted of an offence under section 34 (1) (*b*) below in relation to it.

(4) The reference to a government department in paragraph (*a*) of subsection (1) above includes a reference to a Northern Ireland department.   [**314**]

34. Offences

(1) A person who—

    (*a*) refuses or fails without reasonable cause to comply with a requirement of a preliminary notice under section 28 above;

    (*b*) refuses or fails without reasonable cause to furnish information required under this Part of this Act; or

    (*c*) in furnishing such information makes a statement which he knows to be false in a material particular or recklessly makes a statement which is false in a material particular,

shall be guilty of an offence and liable on summary conviction to a fine not exceeding £400.

(2) Where a person is convicted of an offence under subsection (1) (*b*) above, then, if the default in respect of which he was convicted is continued without reasonable cause after the conviction, he shall be guilty of a further offence and

liable on summary conviction to a fine not exceeding £40 for each day on which the default is continued.

(3) A person who contravenes section 33 above shall be guilty of an offence and liable—

(a) on summary conviction, to a fine not exceeding £200 or to imprisonment for a term not exceeding three months, or to both, and

(b) on conviction on indictment, to imprisonment for a term not exceeding two years or to a fine, or to both.

(4) Summary proceedings for an offence under subsection (1) (c) above may be brought within a period of six months from the date on which evidence sufficient in the opinion of the prosecutor to warrant the proceedings came to his knowledge; but no proceedings shall be brought by virtue of this subsection more than three years after the commission of the offence.

(5) For the purposes of subsection (4) above a certificate signed by or on behalf of the prosecutor and stating the date on which evidence as aforesaid came to his knowledge shall be conclusive evidence of that fact; and a certificate stating that matter and purporting to be so signed shall be deemed to be so signed unless the contrary is proved.

(6) Where an offence under this Part of this Act committed by a body corporate or a Scottish firm is proved to have been committed with the consent or connivance of, or to have been attributable to any neglect on the part of, any director, manager, secretary or other similar officer of the body corporate or firm or a person who was purporting to act in any such capacity, he as well as the body corporate or, as the case may be, the firm shall be guilty of that offence and shall be liable to be proceeded against and punished accordingly.

(7) Where the affairs of a body corporate are managed by its members, subsection (6) above shall apply in relation to the acts and defaults of a member in connection with his functions of management as if he were a director of the body corporate.

(8) Proceedings for an offence under this Part of this Act, other than an offence under subsection (3) above, shall not be instituted—

(a) in England and Wales, except by or with the consent of the Attorney General;

(b) in Northern Ireland except by or with the consent of the Attorney General for Northern Ireland.

(9) Summary proceedings for an offence under this Part of this Act may (without prejudice to any jurisdiction exercisable apart from this subsection) be taken against a body corporate at any place where it has a place of business and against any other person at any place where he is. [**315**]

PART V

GENERAL AND SUPPLEMENTARY

35. Expenses

Any expenses of the Secretary of State or the Minister of Agriculture, Fisheries and Food incurred in consequence of the provisions of this Act, including any increase attributable to those provisions in sums payable under any other Act, shall be defrayed out of money provided by Parliament. [**316**]

36. Service of documents

(1) Any notice or other document required or authorised by or by virtue of this Act to be served on any person may be served on him either by delivering it to him or by leaving it at his proper address or by sending it by post.

(2) Any notice or other document so required or authorised to be served on a body corporate or a firm shall be duly served if it is served on the secretary or clerk of that body or a partner of that firm.

(3) For the purposes of this section, and of section 26 of the Interpretation Act 1889 in its application to this section, the proper address of a person, in the case of a secretary or clerk of a body corporate, shall be that of the registered or principal office of that body, in the case of a partner of a firm shall be that of the principal office of the firm, and in any other case shall be the last known address of the person to be served. [**317**]

37. Interpretation

(1) In this Act, unless the context otherwise requires—

"accounting year", in relation to the Board, means, subject to subsection (2) below, the period of twelve months ending with the 31st December in any year, except that the Board's first accounting year shall end on 31st December 1976;

"enactment" includes an enactment of the Parliament of Northern Ireland or the Northern Ireland Assembly;

"holding company" means a holding company as defined by section 154 of the Companies Act 1948 or section 148 of the Companies Act (Northern Ireland) 1960;

"industry" includes any description of commercial activity, and any section of an industry, and "industrial" has a corresponding meaning;

"manufacturing industry" means, subject to subsection (3) below, activities which are described in any of the minimum list headings in Orders III to XIX (inclusive) of the Standard Industrial Classification;

"the Ministers" means the Secretary of State and the Minister of Agriculture, Fisheries and Food;

"planning agreement" has the meaning assigned to it by section 21 (2) above;

"Standard Industrial Classification" has the meaning assigned to it by section 6 (2) of the Industry Act 1972;

"subsidiary" means a subsidiary as defined by section 154 of the Companies Act 1948 or section 148 of the Companies Act (Northern Ireland) 1960;

"wholly owned subsidiary" has the meaning assigned to it by section 150 (4) of the Companies Act 1948 or section 144 (5) of the Companies Act (Northern Ireland) 1960.

(2) The Secretary of State may direct that any accounting year of the Board shall end on a date before or after that on which it would otherwise end.

(3) In determining the extent to which an undertaking is engaged in manufacturing industry, the following activities shall be treated as manufacturing industry so far as they relate to products manufactured or to be manufactured by the undertaking—

research,

transport,
distribution,
repair and maintenance of machinery,
sales and marketing,
storage,
mining and quarrying,
production and distribution of energy and heating,
administration,
training of staff,
packaging.

(4) Securities and other property are publicly owned for the purposes of this Act if they are held—

(a) by or on behalf of the Crown;

(b) by a company all of whose shares are held by or on behalf of the Crown or by a wholly owned subsidiary of such a company;

(c) by any corporation constituted by or under any enactment under which an industry or part of an industry is carried on by that corporation under national ownership or control; or

(d) by a wholly owned subsidiary of any such corporation.

(5) Except in so far as the context otherwise requires, any reference in this Act to an enactment shall be construed as a reference to that enactment as amended, applied or extended by or under any other enactment, including this Act. [**318**]

38. Orders

(1) Any power to make an order conferred by this Act shall be exercisable by statutory instrument.

(2) Any power to make an order conferred by any provision of this Act shall include power to make an order varying or revoking any order previously made under that provision.

(3) It is hereby declared that any power of giving directions or making determinations conferred on the Secretary of State by any provision of this Act includes power to vary or revoke directions or determinations given or made under that provision. [**319**]

39. Citation etc.

(1) This Act may be cited as the Industry Act 1975.

(2) The enactments specified in Schedule 7 to this Act, not being enactments to which section 22 applies, shall have effect subject to the amendments set out in that Schedule, being amendments consequential on the foregoing provisions of this Act and minor amendments.

(3) The enactments specified in Schedule 8 to this Act are repealed to the extent mentioned in column 3 of that Schedule.

(4) It is hereby declared that this Act extends to Northern Ireland.

(5) Notwithstanding the provisions—

(a) of section 12 (3) of the Statutory Orders (Special Procedure) Act 1945, and

(b) of section 31 (5) of the Trade Union and Labour Relations Act 1974, the former Act shall apply to any compensation order which extends to Northern

Ireland, and the latter Act shall extend to Northern Ireland so far as necessary for the definition of the expression "independent trade union".

(6) This Act shall come into force on such day as the Secretary of State may by order made by statutory instrument appoint.

(7) An order under subsection (6) above may appoint different days for different provisions and for different purposes.   [**320**]

SCHEDULES

SCHEDULE 1

Section 1

The National Enterprise Board

Appointment and tenure of members

1. It shall be the duty of the Secretary of State—

   (*a*) to satisfy himself, before he appoints a person to be a member of the Board, that he will have no such financial or other interest as is likely to affect prejudicially the performance of his functions as a member; and

   (*b*) to satisfy himself from time to time with respect to each member that he has no such interest;

and a person who is a member or whom the Secretary of State proposes to appoint as a member shall, whenever requested by the Secretary of State to do so, furnish the Secretary of State with such information as he may specify with a view to carrying out his duty under this paragraph.

2. Subject to the following provisions of this Schedule, a person shall hold and vacate office as a member or the chairman or a deputy chairman of the Board in accordance with the terms of the instrument appointing him to that office.

3. A person may at any time resign his office as a member or the chairman or a deputy chairman by giving to the Secretary of State a signed notice in writing stating that he resigns that office.

4. Where a member becomes or ceases to be the chairman or a deputy chairman, the Secretary of State may vary the terms of the instrument appointing him a member so as to alter the date on which he is to vacate office as a member.

5. If the chairman or a deputy chairman ceases to be a member, he shall cease to be the chairman or a deputy chairman, as the case may be.

6.—(1) If the Secretary of State is satisfied that a member—

   (*a*) has been absent from meetings of the Board for a period longer than three consecutive months without the permission of the Board; or

   (*b*) has become bankrupt or made an arrangement with his creditors; or

   (*c*) is incapacitated by physical or mental illness; or

   (*d*) is otherwise unable or unfit to discharge the functions of a member,

the Secretary of State may declare his office as a member vacant, and shall notify the declaration in such manner as he thinks fit; and thereupon the office shall become vacant.

(2) In the application of sub-paragraph (1) above to Scotland, for the references in paragraph (*b*) to a member's having become bankrupt and to a member's having made an arrangement with his creditors there shall be substituted respectively a reference to sequestration of a member's estate having been awarded and to a member's having made a trust deed for behoof of his creditors or a composition contract.

[**321**]

Remuneration etc.

7. The Board shall pay to each member such remuneration as the Secretary of State may determine with the approval of the Minister for the Civil Service.

8. The Board shall make such provision as may be determined by the Secretary of State with the approval of the said Minister for the payment of pensions, allowances or gratuities (including refunds of contributions to any pension fund with or without interest or other additions) to or in respect of such members or past members of the Board as may be so determined.

9. Where a person ceases to be a member otherwise than on the expiry of his term of office and it appears to the Secretary of State that there are special circumstances which make it right for that person to receive compensation, the Secretary of State, with the approval of the said Minister, may direct the Board to make to that person a payment of such amount as the Secretary of State may determine with the approval of the said Minister.

10.—(1) Without prejudice to section 2 (3) above, the Board may, in the case of such of the persons employed by them as may be determined by the Board, pay such pensions, allowances or gratuities to or in respect of them as may be so determined, make such payments towards the provision of such pensions, allowances or gratuities (including refunds of contributions to any pension fund with or without interest or other additions) as may be so determined or provide and maintain such schemes (whether contributory or not) for the payment of such pensions, allowances or gratuities as may be so determined.

(2) Where a person employed by the Board and participating in a scheme for the payment of pensions, allowances or gratuities which is applicable to such persons becomes a member of the Board, his service as a member may be treated for the purposes of the scheme as service as a person employed by the Board, whether or not provision for or in respect of him is made under paragraph 8 above. [**322**]

Disqualification of members of the Board for House of Commons

11. In Part II of Schedule 1 to the House of Commons Disqualification Act 1975 and in Part II of Schedule 1 to the Northern Ireland Assembly Disqualification Act 1975 (bodies of which all members are disqualified), there shall be inserted, at the appropriate place in alphabetical order:—

"The National Enterprise Board".   [**323**]

Proceedings

12. The quorum of the Board and the arrangements relating to meetings of the Board shall be such as the Board may determine.

13.—(1) A member who is in any way directly or indirectly interested in a contract made or proposed to be made by the Board, or in any other matter whatsoever which falls to be considered by the Board, shall disclose the nature of his interest at a meeting of the Board and the disclosure shall be recorded in the minutes of the meeting.

(2) The member shall not—

    (a) in the case of any such contract, take part in any deliberation or decision of the Board with respect to the contract; and

    (b) in the case of any other matter, take part in any deliberation or decision of the Board with respect to the matter if the Board decide that the interest in question might prejudicially affect the member's consideration of the matter.

(3) For the purposes of this paragraph, a notice given by a member at a meeting of the Board to the effect that he is a member of a specified body corporate or firm

and is to be regarded as interested in any contract which is made with the body corporate or firm after the date of the notice, and in any other matter whatsoever concerning the body corporate or firm which falls to be considered by the Board after that date, shall be a sufficient disclosure of his interest.

(4) A member need not attend in person at a meeting of the Board in order to make a disclosure which he is required to make under this paragraph, if he takes reasonable steps to secure that the disclosure is made by a notice which is taken into consideration and read at such a meeting.

14. The validity of any proceedings of the Board shall not be affected by any vacancy among the members or by any defect in the appointment of a member or by any failure to comply with the requirements of paragraph 13 above.   [**324**]

Incorporation of Board and Execution of Instruments and Contracts

15. The Board shall be a body corporate.

16. The fixing of the common seal shall be authenticated by the signature of the secretary of the Board or some other person authorised by the Board to act for that purpose.

17. A document purporting to be duly executed under the seal of the Board shall be received in evidence and shall be deemed to be so executed unless the contrary is proved.   [**325**]

Stamp Duty

18.—(1) Stamp duty shall not be chargeable on any instrument which is certified to the Commissioners of Inland Revenue by the Board as having been made or executed for the purpose of the transfer to the Board of securities or other property held—

    (a) by or on behalf of the Crown; or
    (b) by a company all of whose shares are held by or on behalf of the Crown or by a wholly owned subsidiary of such a company.

(2) Stamp duty shall not be chargeable on any vesting order or on any instrument for giving effect to such an order.

(3) No such order or instrument as is mentioned in sub-paragraph (1) or (2) above shall be deemed to be duly stamped unless it is stamped with the duty for which it would but for this paragraph be liable or it has, in accordance with the provisions of section 12 of the Stamp Act 1891, been stamped with a particular stamp denoting that it is not chargeable with any duty or that it is duly stamped.
[**326**]

Acquisition of holdings of minority shareholders

19. Section 209 of the Companies Act 1948 (power to acquire shares of shareholders dissenting from scheme or contract approved by majority) shall have effect in relation to the transfer of shares or any class of shares in a company to the Board; and references to a transferee company in that section shall be construed accordingly.
[**327**]

Circulars

20. Section 14 (1) of the Prevention of Fraud (Investments) Act 1958 and section 13 (1) of the Prevention of Fraud (Investments) Act (Northern Ireland) 1940 (prohibition on distributing circulars relating to investments) shall not apply to documents which the Board distribute in the discharge of their functions or cause to be so distributed or have in their possession for the purposes of such distribution.
[**328**]

SCHEDULE 2

Financial and Administrative Provisions Relating to Board

Borrowing Powers

1.—(1) The Board may borrow money only—

(a) in accordance with sub-paragraphs (2) and (3) below, or

(b) from their wholly-owned subsidiaries.

(2) The Board may borrow temporarily, by way of overdraft or otherwise, such sums as they may require for meeting their obligations and discharging their functions—

(a) in sterling from the Secretary of State, or

(b) with the consent of the Secretary of State and the approval of the Treasury, or in accordance with any general authority given by the Secretary of State with the approval of the Treasury, either in sterling or in a currency other than sterling from a person other than the Secretary of State.

(3) The Board may borrow otherwise than by way of temporary loan such sums as they may require for capital purposes or for fulfilling guarantees entered into by them—

(a) in sterling from the Secretary of State, or

(b) with the consent of the Secretary of State and the approval of the Treasury, in sterling from the Commission of the European Communities or the European Investment Bank, or

(c) with the like consent and approval, in any currency other than sterling from a person other than the Secretary of State.

(4) References to borrowing in this paragraph do not include borrowing under section 3 above. **[329]**

Government loans to the Board

2.—(1) The Secretary of State may lend to the Board any sums which the Board have power to borrow from him under paragraph 1 above, and the Treasury may issue to the Secretary of State out of the National Loans Fund any sum necessary to enable the Secretary of State to make loans in pursuance of this sub-paragraph.

(2) Any loans made in pursuance of sub-paragraph (1) above shall be repaid to the Secretary of State at such times and by such methods, and interest on the loans shall be paid to him at such times and at such rates, as he may from time to time direct; and all sums received by the Secretary of State in pursuance of this sub-paragraph shall be paid into the National Loans Fund.

(3) The Secretary of State shall prepare in respect of each financial year an account of the sums issued to him in pursuance of sub-paragraph (1) above and the sums received by him in pursuance of sub-paragraph (2) above and of the disposal by him of those sums and shall send the account to the Comptroller and Auditor General before the end of the month of November next following the end of that year; and the Comptroller and Auditor General shall examine, certify and report on the account and lay copies of it and of his report before each House of Parliament.

(4) The Secretary of State shall not make a loan or give a direction in pursuance of this paragraph except with the approval of the Treasury; and the form of the account prepared in pursuance of sub-paragraph (3) above and the manner of preparing it shall be such as the Treasury may direct. **[330]**

Borrowing by wholly owned subsidiaries

3. It shall be the duty of the Board to secure that no wholly owned subsidiary of theirs borrows money otherwise than from the Board or from another wholly

owned subsidiary of theirs except with the consent of the Secretary of State and the approval of the Treasury. [**331**]

Guarantees

4.—(1) The Treasury may guarantee, in such manner and on such conditions as they think fit, the repayment of the principal of and the payment of interest on any sums which the Board borrow from a person other than the Secretary of State.

(2) Immediately after a guarantee is given under this paragraph the Treasury shall lay a statement of the guarantee before each House of Parliament; and where any sum is issued for fulfilling a guarantee so given, the Treasury shall lay before each House of Parliament a statement relating to that sum, as soon as possible after the end of each financial year, beginning with that in which the sum is issued and ending with that in which all liability in respect of the principal of the sum and in respect of interest on it is finally discharged.

(3) Any sums required by the Treasury for fulfilling a guarantee under this paragraph shall be charged on and issued out of the Consolidated Fund.

(4) If any sums are issued in fulfilment of a guarantee given under this paragraph, the Board shall make to the Treasury, at such time and in such manner as the Treasury from time to time direct, payments of such amounts as the Treasury so direct in or towards repayment of the sums so issued and payments of interest, at such rate as the Treasury so direct, on what is outstanding for the time being in respect of sums so issued.

(5) Any sums received by the Treasury in pursuance of sub-paragraph (4) above shall be paid into the Consolidated Fund. [**332**]

Other Government investment in the Board

5.—(1) The Secretary of State may pay to the Board out of money provided by Parliament such sums (in this Schedule referred to as "public dividend capital") as the Secretary of State thinks fit.

(2) The Secretary of State may direct that so much of the debt assumed by the Board under paragraph 6 below as he may, with the approval of the Treasury, determine shall be treated as an addition to that capital.

(3) In consideration of receiving public dividend capital the Board shall make to the Secretary of State, as respect each accounting year (except such a year as respects which the Board satisfy the Secretary of State that it is inappropriate to make a payment in pursuance of this sub-paragraph), payments of such amounts as may be proposed by the Board and agreed by the Secretary of State or such other amounts as the Secretary of State may determine, after consultation with the Board; and any sums received by the Secretary of State in pursuance of this sub-paragraph shall be paid into the Consolidated Fund.

(4) The account prepared in respect of any financial year in pursuance of paragraph 2 (3) above shall include particulars of the sums which in that year are paid to the Board or are paid into the Consolidated Fund in pursuance of this paragraph.

(5) The Secretary of State shall not make a payment, signify agreement or make a determination in pursuance of this paragraph except with the approval of the Treasury. [**333**]

The Board's Capital Debt

6.—(1) Upon any acquisition to which this paragraph applies, the Board shall assume a debt to the Secretary of State of such amount as may be notified to the Board in writing by him, with the approval of the Treasury.

(2) This paragraph applies to any acquisition by the Board—
  (*a*) of securities or other property held—
    (i) by or on behalf of the Crown; or
    (ii) by a company all of whose shares are held by or on behalf of the Crown or by a wholly owned subsidiary of such a company; or
  (*b*) under section 3 above; or
  (*c*) under a vesting order.

(3) Subject to sub-paragraph (4) below, in a case to which sub-paragraph (2) (*a*) above applies the amount to be notified is the aggregate of the following, namely—
  (*a*) the consideration given when the property was first brought into public ownership, and
  (*b*) the costs and expenses of and incidental to it being brought into public ownership.

(4) If it appears to the Secretary of State in any such case that there has been such a change in circumstances since the property was first brought into public ownership that its true value would not be reflected by reference to the consideration mentioned in sub-paragraph (3) above, the Secretary of State, with the approval of the Treasury, shall determine the amount to be notified.

(5) In a case to which sub-paragraph (2) (*b*) above applies, the amount to be notified is the aggregate of the consideration for the acquisition and the costs and expenses of and incidental to it.

(6) In a case to which sub-paragraph (2) (c) above applies, the amount is the aggregate of the compensation under the relevant compensation order and the costs and expenses of and incidental to the acquisition.

(7) The rate of interest payable on so much of the Board's capital debt as the Secretary of State does not direct to be treated as an addition to the Board's public dividend capital, and the date from which interest is to begin to accrue, the arrangements for paying off the principal, and the other terms of the debt shall be such as the Secretary of State, with the approval of the Treasury, may from time to time determine; and different rates and dates may be determined under this sub-paragraph with respect to different portions of the debt.

(8) Any sums received by the Secretary of State under sub-paragraph (7) above shall be paid into the National Loans Fund. [**334**]

Accounts and audit

7.—(1) The Board shall keep proper accounts and proper records in relation to the accounts and shall prepare in respect of each accounting year a statement of accounts in such form as the Secretary of State, with the approval of the Treasury, may direct, being a form which shall conform to the best commercial standards.

(2) The accounts and statements of accounts of the Board (other than interim statements under sub-paragraph (4) below) shall be audited by auditors appointed by the Board after consultation with the Secretary of State, and a person shall not be qualified to be so appointed unless he is a member of one or more of the following bodies—

The Institute of Chartered Accountants in England and Wales;
The Institute of Chartered Accountants of Scotland;
The Association of Certified Accountants;
The Institute of Chartered Accountants in Ireland;
any other body of accountants established in the United Kingdom and for the time being recognised for the purposes of section 161 (1) (*a*) of the Companies Act 1948 or section 155 (1) (*a*) of the Companies Act (Northern Ireland) 1960;

but a Scottish firm may be so appointed if each of the partners is qualified to be appointed.

(3) As soon as the accounts and statement of accounts of the Board for any accounting year have been audited under sub-paragraph (2) above, the Board shall send to the Secretary of State a copy of the statement together with a copy of any report made by the auditor on that statement or on the accounts of the Board.

(4) The Board shall also prepare in respect of the first six months of each accounting year an interim statement of accounts in such form as the Secretary of State, with the approval of the Treasury, may direct, and shall do so as soon as practicable after the end of the period to which the statement relates.

(5) As soon as an interim statement of accounts has been prepared, the Board shall send a copy of the statement to the Secretary of State.

(6) It shall be the duty of the Secretary of State to lay before each House of Parliament a copy of every statement and report of which a copy is received by him under this paragraph. [**335**]

Annual report

8.—(1) It shall be the duty of the Board to make to the Secretary of State as soon as possible after the end of each accounting year, a report dealing with the operations of the Board during that year.

(2) It shall be the duty of the Secretary of State to lay before each House of Parliament a copy of each report received by him under this paragraph.

(3) A copy of the register under section 1 (8) above, as amended from time to time, shall be annexed to each such report.

(4) If a report laid before Parliament under sub-paragraph (2) above sets out a direction under section 7 above a copy of which has not been laid in accordance with subsection (3) of that section, a statement of the reason why the copy was not so laid shall be annexed to the report by the Secretary of State, and the said subsection (3) shall not apply to the direction. [**336**]

SCHEDULE 3

Section 20

ARBITRATION

PART I

GENERAL

Establishment of Tribunal

1. If a party to a dispute such as is mentioned in subsection (1) of section 20 above serves on the other party or parties to the dispute, at a time when no proceedings relating to it have been commenced in any court, a notice that he wishes the dispute to be determined by arbitration, the Secretary of State shall by order establish a tribunal to determine the dispute and any other dispute such as is mentioned in subsection (2) of that section.

2. An order under paragraph 1 above shall be laid before each House of Parliament.

3. A tribunal shall be a court of record and shall have an official seal which shall be judicially noticed.

4. A tribunal shall, as the Lord Chancellor may direct, either sit as a single tribunal or sit in two or more divisions and, subject to paragraph 5 below, shall, for the hearing of any proceedings, consist of—

    (a) a president who shall be a barrister or solicitor of at least seven years standing appointed by the Lord Chancellor, and (*b*) two other members appointed by the Secretary of State, one being a person of experience in business and the other being a person of experience in finance.

5. In its application to proceedings which, by virtue of paragraph 18 below, are to be treated as Scottish proceedings, paragraph 4 above shall have effect with the substitution, for sub-paragraph (*a*) thereof, of the following sub-paragraph—

"(*a*) a president who shall be an advocate or solicitor who has practised in Scotland and who shall be appointed by the Lord President of the Court of Session".

6. The members of a tribunal shall hold office for such period as may be determined at the time of their respective appointments and shall be eligible for reappointment but, notwithstanding that the period for which a member was appointed has not expired—

(*a*) a member may, at any time by not less than one month's notice in writing to his appointor, resign his office;

(*b*) the appointor of a member may declare the office of that member vacant on the ground that he is unfit to continue in his office; and

(*c*) if any member becomes bankrupt or makes a composition with creditors or, in Scotland, if sequestration of a member's estate is awarded or a member makes a trust deed for behoof of his creditors or a composition contract, his office shall thereupon become vacant.

7. If any member of a tribunal becomes, by reason of illness or other infirmity, temporarily incapable of performing the duties of his office, his appointor shall appoint some other fit person to discharge his duties for any period not exceeding 6 months at any one time, and the person so appointed shall during that period have the same powers as the person in whose place he was appointed.

8. In this Part of this Schedule, "appointor", in relation to a member of a tribunal means—

(*a*) in the case of a member appointed under sub-paragraph (*a*) of paragraph 4 above, the Lord Chancellor or, if paragraph 5 above applies, the Lord President of the Court of Session; and

(*b*) in the case of any other member, the Secretary of State.

9. In Part II of Schedule 1 to the House of Commons Disqualification Act 1975 and in Part II of Schedule 1 to the Northern Ireland Assembly Disqualification Act 1975 (bodies of which all members are disqualified), there shall be inserted, at the appropriate place in alphabetical order:—

"An Arbitration Tribunal established under Schedule 3 to the Industry Act 1975".

10. In Part I of Schedule 1 to the Tribunals and Inquiries Act 1971 (Tribunals under direct supervision of Council on Tribunals) after the entry the first column of which reads "Indemnification of justices and clerks" here shall be inserted the following entry—

"Industry. 9A. An arbitration tribunal established under Schedule 3 to the Industry Act 1975." [**337**]

Staff and expenses

11. A tribunal may appoint such officers as they consider necessary for assisting them in the proper execution of their duties.

12.—(1) There shall be paid to members of a tribunal such remuneration (whether by way of salaries or fees) and such allowances as the Secretary of State may, with the approval of the Minister for the Civil Service, determine.

(2) There shall be paid to any officer appointed under paragraph 11 above and any person to whom proceedings are referred by the tribunal under paragraph 27

below for inquiry and report such remuneration (whether by way of salary or fees) and such allowances as the tribunal may, with the approval of the Secretary of State given with the consent of the Minister for the Civil Service, determine.

(3) The Secretary of State shall pay any such remuneration and allowances and any other expenses of a tribunal shall be defrayed by the Secretary of State out of money provided by Parliament. [**338**]

PART II
PROCEEDINGS
Proceedings other than Scottish proceedings

13. Paragraphs 14 to 17 below shall have effect with respect to proceedings of a tribunal other than those which, by virtue of paragraph 18 below, are to be treated as Scottish proceedings.

14. The provisions of the Arbitration Act 1950 or, in Northern Ireland, the Arbitration Act (Northern Ireland) 1937 with respect to—

(*a*) the administration of oaths and the taking of affirmations,
(*b*) the correction in awards of mistakes and errors,
(*c*) the summoning, attendance and examination of witnesses and the production of documents, and
(*d*) the costs of the reference and award,

shall, with any necessary modifications, apply in respect of such proceedings but, except as provided by this paragraph, the provisions of that Act shall not apply to any such proceedings.

15. A tribunal may, and if so ordered by the Court of Appeal shall, state in the form of a special case for determination by the Court of Appeal any question of law which may arise in such proceedings.

16. An appeal shall lie to the Court of Appeal on any question of law or fact from any determination or order of the tribunal with respect to compensation under section 16 (5) above.

17.—(1) Subject to the provisions of this Schedule, the procedure in or in connection with any such proceedings shall be such as may be determined by rules made by the Lord Chancellor by statutory instrument.

(2) A statutory instrument containing rules made under this paragraph shall be subject to annulment in pursuance of a resolution of either House of Parliament.
[**339**]

Scottish proceedings

18. Where a dispute submitted to a tribunal relates to capital of a body corporate whose principal place of business is situated in Scotland, or assets which are situated in Scotland, then, subject to paragraph 20 below, the proceedings before the tribunal in respect of the dispute shall be treated as Scottish proceedings.

19. If, at any stage in any proceedings before a tribunal which would not otherwise fall to be treated as Scottish proceedings, the tribunal are satisfied that, by reason of the fact that questions of Scottish law arise or for any other reason, the proceedings ought thereafter to be treated as Scottish proceedings, the tribunal may order that they shall thereafter be so treated and the provisions of this Schedule shall have effect accordingly.

20. If, at any stage in any proceedings before a tribunal which would otherwise be treated as Scottish proceedings, the tribunal are satisfied that, by reason of the fact that questions of English law arise or for any other reason, the proceedings

ought not to be treated as Scottish proceedings, they may make an order that the proceedings shall thereafter not be treated as Scottish proceedings and the proceedings of this Schedule shall have effect accordingly.

21. In Scottish proceedings a tribunal shall have the like powers for securing the attendance of witnesses and the production of documents and with regard to the examination of witnesses on oath and the awarding of expenses as if the tribunal were an arbiter under a submission.

22. A tribunal may and if so directed by the Court of Session shall state a case for the opinion of that Court on any question of law arising in Scottish proceedings.

23.—(1) An appeal shall lie to the Court of Session on any question of law or fact from any determination or order of the tribunal with respect to compensation under section 16 (6) above.

(2) An appeal shall lie, with the leave of the Court of Session or of the House of Lords, from any decision of the Court of Session under this paragraph, and such leave may be given on such terms as to costs or otherwise as the Court of Session or the House of Lords may determine.

24.—(1) Subject to the provisions of this Schedule, the procedure in or in connection with Scottish proceedings shall be such as may be determined by rules made by the Lord Advocate by statutory instrument.

(2) A statutory instrument containing rules made under this paragraph shall be subject to annulment in pursuance of a resolution of either House of Parliament.

25. Unless the tribunal consider that there are special reasons for not doing so, they shall sit in Scotland for the hearing and determination of any Scottish proceedings. [**340**]

All proceedings

26. Every order of a tribunal—

(a) shall be enforceable in England and Wales and Northern Ireland as if it were an order of the High Court; and

(b) may be recorded for execution in the books of Council and Session and may be enforced accordingly.

27. A tribunal may, at any stage in any proceedings before them, refer to a person or persons appointed by them for the purpose any question arising in the proceedings, other than a question which in their opinion is primarily one of law, for inquiry and report, and the report of any such person or persons may be adopted wholly or partly by the tribunal and, if so adopted, may be incorporated in an order of the tribunal. [**341**]

SCHEDULE 4

Section 22

AMENDMENTS TO PART II OF INDUSTRY ACT 1972

PART I

AMENDMENTS EXTENDING POWERS TO GIVE SELECTIVE FINANCIAL ASSISTANCE UNDER INDUSTRY ACT 1972

1. The following provisions of section 7 (selective financial assistance for industry in assisted areas) of the Industry Act 1972 are repealed, namely—

(a) the words in subsection (4) from the beginning to "and" (which restrict the power to give assistance by means of investment by acquisition of loan

or share capital to cases where the Secretary of State is satisfied that
financial assistance cannot, or cannot appropriately, be given in any other
way); and

(b) subsection (5) (which requires the Secretary of State to dispose of shares
or stock as soon as, in his opinion, it is reasonably practicable to do so).

2. The following provisions of section 8 of that Act (general powers of selective
financial assistance) are repealed, namely—

(a) subsection (1) (c) (which prevents the exercise of the powers conferred by
the section unless financial assistance cannot, or cannot appropriately, be
provided otherwise than by the Secretary of State);

(b) in subsection (3)—

(i) the words from the beginning to "and", in the first place where it
occurs, (which correspond to the words in section 7 (4) repealed by
paragraph 1 (a) above); and

(ii) paragraph (b) (which prevents the Secretary of State, in exercise of
his powers under the section, acquiring more than half, by nominal
value, of the equity share capital of any company);

(c) subsection (4) (which corresponds to section 7 (5)); and

(d) subsection (5) (which limits the duration of the Secretary of State's powers
under the section, except so far as relates to the making of a payment in
pursuance of an undertaking previously given, to the period ending 31st
December 1977).   [**342**]

Minor and consequential amendments to Part II of Industry Act 1972

3. In section 7 (4) of that Act (selective financial assistance for industry in
assisted areas), for the words "so described" there shall be substituted the words
"described in subsection (3) (a) above".

4. In section 8 (3) of that Act (selective financial assistance: general powers),
for the words "so described" there shall be substituted the words "described in
subsection (3) (a) of the last preceding section".

5. The following subsection shall be added at the end of section 9 of that Act
(Industrial Development Advisory Board)—

"(5) Any reference in this section to the Secretary of State's functions
under sections 7 and 8 of this Act includes a reference to his functions under
section 3 of the Industry Act 1975."   [**343**]

PART II.

PART II OF INDUSTRY ACT 1972 AS AMENDED BY THIS ACT

PART II

FINANCIAL ASSISTANCE FOR INDUSTRY

7. Selective financial assistance for industry in assisted areas

(1) For the purposes set out in the following provisions of this section the Secretary
of State may, with the consent of the Treasury, provide financial assistance where,
in his opinion—

(a) the financial assistance is likely to provide, maintain or safeguard employment in any part of the assisted areas, and

(b) the undertakings for which the assistance is provided are or will be wholly
or mainly in the assisted areas.

(2) The purposes mentioned in subsection (1) of this section are—

(*a*) to promote the development or modernisation of an industry,

(*b*) to promote the efficiency of an industry,

(*c*) to create, expand or sustain productive capacity in an industry, or in undertakings in an industry,

(*d*) to promote the reconstruction, reorganisation or conversion of an industry or of undertakings in an industry,

(*e*) to encourage the growth of, or the proper distribution of undertakings in, an industry,

(*f*) to encourage arrangements for ensuring that any contraction of an industry proceeds in an orderly way.

(3) Subject to the following provisions of this section, financial assistance under this section may be given on any terms or conditions, and by any description of investment or lending or guarantee, or by making grants, and may, in particular, be—

(*a*) investment by acquisition of loan or share capital in any company, including an acquisition effected by the Secretary of State through another company, being a company formed for the purpose of giving financial assistance under this Part of this Act,

(*b*) investment by the acquisition of any undertaking or of any assets,

(*c*) a loan, whether secured or unsecured, and whether or not carrying interest, or interest at a commercial rate,

(*d*) any form of insurance or guarantee to meet any contingency, and in particular to meet default on payment of a loan, or of interest on a loan, or non-fulfilment of a contract.

(4) The Secretary of State, in giving financial assistance in the way described in subsection (3) (*a*) above shall not acquire any shares or stock in a company without the consent of that company.

(5) . . .

(6) In this section "industry", unless the context otherwise requires, includes any description of commercial activity, and references to an industry include references to any section of an industry.

(7) In this section "the assisted areas" means the development areas, the intermediate areas and Northern Ireland.

8. Selective financial assistance: General powers

(1) For the purposes set out in subsection (2) of the last preceding section the Secretary of State may, with the consent of the Treasury, provide financial assistance where, in his opinion—

(*a*) the financial assistance is likely to benefit the economy of the United Kingdom, or of any part or area of the United Kingdom, and

(*b*) it is in the national interest that the financial assistance should be provided on the scale, and in the form and manner, proposed.

(*c*) . . .

(2) Financial assistance under this section may, subject to the following provisions of this section, be given in any of the ways set out in subsection (3) of the last preceding section.

(3) The Secretary of State, in giving financial assistance in the way described in subsection (3) (*a*) of the last preceding section—

(*a*) shall not acquire any shares or stock in a company without the consent of that company,

(*b*) . . .

(4) . . .

(5) . . .

(6) The aggregate of—

(*a*) the sums paid by the Secretary of State under this section, plus

(*b*) the liabilities of the Secretary of State under any guarantees given by him under this section (exclusive of any liability in respect of interest on a principal sum so guaranteed),

less any sum received by the Secretary of State by way of repayment of loans under this section, or repayment of principal sums paid to meet a guarantee under this section, shall not at any time exceed the limit specified in subsection (7) below.

(7) The said limit shall be £150 million, but the Secretary of State may, on not more than four occasions, by order made with the consent of the Treasury increase or further increase that limit by a sum specified in the order, being a sum not exceeding £100 million.

An order under this subsection shall be contained in a statutory instrument, and such an order shall not be made unless a draft of the order has been approved by a resolution of the Commons House of Parliament.

(8) The sums which the Secretary of State pays or undertakes to pay by way of financial assistance under this section in respect of any one project shall not exceed £5 million, except so far as any excess over the said sum of £5 million has been authorised by a resolution of the Commons House of Parliament:

Provided that this subsection shall not apply where the Secretary of State is satisfied that the payment or undertaking is urgently needed at a time when it is impracticable to obtain the approval of the Commons House of Parliament; and in that case the Secretary of State shall lay a statement concerning the financial assistance before each House of Parliament.

9. Industrial Development Advisory Board

(1) The Secretary of State shall appoint a board, which shall be called the Industrial Development Advisory Board, to advise him with respect to the exercise of his functions under sections 7 and 8 of this Act.

(2) The Board shall consist of a chairman and not less than six nor more than twelve other members.

(3) The members of the Board shall include persons who appear to the Secretary of State to have wide experience of, and to have shown capacity in, industry, banking, accounting and finance.

(4) If the Board make a recommendation with respect to any matter at the request of the Secretary of State and the Secretary of State exercises his functions under sections 7 and 8 of this Act contrary to their recommendation, he shall, if the Board so request, lay a statement as to the matter before Parliament.

(5) Any reference in this section to the Secretary of State's functions under sections 7 and 8 of this Act includes a reference to his functions under section 3 of the Industry Act 1975. [**344**]

SCHEDULE 5

Section 27

DISCLOSURE OF INFORMATION BY GOVERNMENT

1. For the purposes of this Schedule the Treasury shall keep a macro-economic model suitable for demonstrating the likely effects on economic events in the United Kingdom of different assumptions about the following matters, namely—

(*a*) government economic policies;

(*b*) economic events outside the United Kingdom; and

(*c*) such (if any) other matters as appear to the Treasury from time to time likely to have a substantial effect on economic events in the United Kingdom.

2. The model shall enable forecasts to be made—
   (*a*) of any of the following, namely—
       (i) the level of growth domestic product;
       (ii) unemployment;
       (iii) the balance of payments on current account;
       (iv) the general index of retail prices; and
       (v) average earnings; and
   (*b*) of such (if any) other economic variables as are appropriate in the opinion of the Treasury from time to time.

3. The references to forecasts in paragraphs 2 above are references to forecasts relating to successive periods of three months and not to shorter periods.

4. The model shall be maintained on a computer.

5. The model shall be available to members of the public to make forecasts based on their own assumptions, using the computer during office hours upon payment of such reasonable fee as the Treasury may determine.

6. Nor less than twice in each year commencing with a date not later than one year from the coming into force of this Act, the Treasury shall publish forecasts produced with the aid of the model as to such matters and based on such alternative assumptions as appear to them to be appropriate.

7. Any forecast under this Schedule shall indicate, where possible, the margin of error attaching to it.

8. The Treasury shall from time to time publish an analysis of errors in such forecasts that would have remained even if the assumptions set out in the forecasts and on which they were based had been correct.

9. It shall be the duty of a Minister of the Crown who proposes to enter into, or has entered into a planning agreement with a body corporate to participate with that body in demonstrating so far as possible, upon the application of that body, the relationship between the undertaking to which the agreement relates and the national economy. [**345**]

SCHEDULE 6

Section 32

ADVISORY COMMITTEES

1. The Secretary of State, with the consent of the Ministry of Agriculture, Fisheries and Food, shall draw up and from time to time revise—
   (*a*) a panel of persons who have experience in industrial affairs as employers or managers;
   (*b*) a panel of persons who have experience in industrial affairs as representatives of workers;
   (*c*) a panel of persons who are barristers or solicitors; and
   (*d*) a panel of persons who are advocates or solicitors who have practised in Scotland.

2. Of the panels—
   (*a*) that mentioned in paragraph 1 (*c*) above shall be appointed with the consent of the Lord Chancellor, and
   (*b*) that mentioned in paragraph 1 (*d*) above shall be appointed with the consent of Lord President of the Court of Session.

3. When either of the Ministers is required to make a reference under section 32 above or makes such a reference himself, he shall constitute, for the purpose of advising him, a committee consisting of three persons, namely—
   (*a*) one from the panel mentioned in paragraph 1 (*a*) above,

(b) one from the panel mentioned in paragraph 1 (b) above, and
(c) one from the relevant panel of lawyers;

and for the purposes of this Schedule, "the relevant panel of lawyers" means—

(i) the panel mentioned in paragraph 1 (d) above, if the Minister constituting the committee considers, having regard to any representations made by the company or companies concerned or by the authorised representative of a relevant trade union, that this is appropriate, and
(ii) in any other case, the panel mentioned in paragraph 1 (c) above.

4. The Minister constituting a committee shall appoint as the committee's chairman the member of the committee appointed to it from the relevant panel of lawyers.

5. A committee may, at the discretion of the chairman, where it appears expedient to do so, call in the aid of one or more persons who appear to the committee to be specially qualified for the purpose, and may settle its advice wholly or partly with the assistance of that person or persons.

6. A committee shall sit in private.

7. The Minister appointing a committee shall pay its expenses, including such (if any) fees for its members and for any person called in under paragraph 5 above as he may, with the approval of the Minister for the Civil Service, determine.

8. Any such Minister may make arrangements for securing that such of his officers as he considers are required are available to assist a committee.

9.—(1) The Secretary of State may make regulations as to the procedure for or in connection with references by advisory committees and the making by such committees of reports to the Minister concerning such references.

(2) Without prejudice to the generality of sub-paragraph (1) above, the regulations may prescribe the time within which representations are to be made.

(3) Regulations under this paragraph shall be made by statutory instrument.

(4) A statutory instrument containing regulations under this paragraph shall be subject to annulment in pursuance of a resolution of either House of Parliament.

[**346**]

SCHEDULE 7

Section 39

MINOR AND CONSEQUENTIAL AMENDMENTS OF INDUSTRY ACT 1972

1. In section 6 (2) of the Industry Act 1972 (interpretation of Part I) the words "or a pipe-line" shall be omitted from the definitions of "machinery or plant" and "works" (where their inclusion has the effect of making capital expenditure on machinery or plant consisting of a pipe-line ineligible for regional development grant).

2. At the end of section 16 (1) (a) of that Act (annual reports of Secretary of State) there shall be added the words "and section 3 of the Industry Act 1975".

[**347**]

SCHEDULE 8

REPEALS

Chapter	Short Title	Extent of Repeal
1972 c. 63	The Industry Act 1972	In section 6 (2), in the definition of "machinery or plant" the words "or a pipe-line"; the definition of "pipe-line" and in the definition of "works" the words "or a pipe-line". In section 7, in subsection (4) the words from the beginning to "and" and subsection (5). In section 8, in subsection (1) paragraph (c) and the word "and" immediately preceding it, in subsection (3) the words from the beginning to "and" in the first place where it occurs and paragraph (b) and the word "and" immediately preceding it, and subsections (4) and (5).

APPENDIX

NATIONAL ENTERPRISE BOARD INVESTMENTS

as at 31st August 1976

Company and Description of Shares		% Share-holding	Cost £000
Anglo Venezuelan Railway Corporation:			
3,500	£1 Ordinary Shares	35·00	3
British Leyland Limited:			
246,490,683	50p Ordinary Shares	95·07	246,491
Brown Boveri Kent Limited:			
7,658,938	25p Ordinary Shares	17·65	1,880
Cambridge Instruments Limited:			
4,261,757	10p Ordinary Shares ⎫		
37,684,255	1p Ordinary Shares ⎬	28·26	1,250
Data Recording Instrument Company Limited:			
2,400,000	£1 Ordinary Shares	53·93	2,407
Dunford & Elliott Limited:			
271,357	25p Ordinary Voting Shares ..	2·57	122
Ferranti Limited:			
4,000,000	50p Ordinary Voting Shares ⎫		
2,666,666	50p Ordinary Non-voting Shares ⎬	62·50	8,667
Herbert Limited:			
43,632,948	25p Ordinary Shares	100·00	26,180
International Computer (Holdings) Limited:			
8,148,750	£1 Ordinary Shares	24·42	12,083
Rolls-Royce (1971) Limited:			
168,000,000	£1 Ordinary Shares	100·00	168,000
			£467,083

INDEX

References in this index are to paragraph numbers.

ADVISORY COMMITTEE,
 disclosure of information to trade unions,
  reference to, 240, 262–265, 313, 346
ARBITRATION,
 tribunal—
  appeal, 206, 339
   Scottish proceedings, 340
  compensation or vesting order, disputes as to, 206, 301, 337
  establishment, 337
  members, 207, 337
  order, enforceability, 341
  proceedings, 207, 339
   Scottish, 339
  questions of fact, reference, 341
  staff and expenses, 337
  vesting or compensation order, as to,
   189, 206, 207, 301, 337–341
  tribunal, submission to, 206, 301, 337,
   and see tribunal *supra.*
ASSISTED AREAS,
 financial assistance under 1972 Act, s. 7
  in, 73, 75, 232, 344. *See also*
  INDUSTRY ACT, 1972
 meaning, 80, 232, 344
 planning agreements, references to, 223,
  224

BOARD. *See* NATIONAL ENTERPRISE
 BOARD
BODY CORPORATE. *See* COMPANY
BROADCASTING,
 interests in, limits on Board's powers,
  64, 65, 67, 290

COMPANY,
 creditors, financial liability of Government to, 98 *et seq.*
 disclosure of information, 240 *et seq.*, 309
  et seq.
  Minister, by, 240, 275 *et seq.*, 308, 345
  offences, 273, 315
  relevant trade unions, to, 240, 244,
   246, 257 *et seq.*, 309, 312, 313
 financial assistance under 1972 Act.
  See INDUSTRY ACT, 1972
 foreign takeover of important manufacturing undertaking, powers, 151 *et
  seq.*, 292. *See also* MANUFACTURING
  UNDERTAKING

COMPANY—*contd.*
 holding, meaning, 318
 loan capital, vesting order on foreign
  takeover. *See* MANUFACTURING
  UNDERTAKING
 planning agreements. *See* PLANNING
  AGREEMENTS
 securities. *See* SECURITIES
 service of documents, 317
 share capital—
  Board, acquisition by—
   holdings of minority shareholders,
    44, 327
   limits, 43–49, 291
  vesting order to prevent foreign takeover. *See* MANUFACTURING
   UNDERTAKING
 shares. *See* SECURITIES
 shipbuilding. *See* SHIPBUILDING
 subsidiary, meaning, 318
 wholly owned subsidiary, meaning, 318
COMPENSATION ORDER,
 foreign takeover of important manufacturing undertaking, prevention,
  152, 178, 184, 189–207. *See also*
  MANUFACTURING UNDERTAKING
COMPULSORY ACQUISITION,
 manufacturing undertaking, on attempted foreign takeover of, 152, 173,
  294–297, 301
CORPORATION. *See* COMPANY
CROWN,
 Board not regarded as agent of, 24, 283
 privilege, inapplicable to Board, 24, 283
 securities and property held by, 51, 318
  acquisition by Board, 35, 51, 284
  capital debt, 334
 property, transfer to Board, stamp duty,
  26, 326

DEVELOPMENT AREA,
 Act of 1972, s. 7, assisted area under, 80,
  344
 regional development grant, 232
DEVELOPMENT OF INVENTIONS ACT,
 1967,
 amendment, 114, 148, 149, 307
 N.R.D.C., activities requiring Ministerial
  approval, 150
 limit raised, 149, 307

References are to paragraph numbers

References are to paragraph numbers

References are to paragraph numbers

Index

MANUFACTURING UNDERTAKING
—cont.
foreign takeover—*cont.*
vesting order—*cont.*
    charging rights etc. to compensation, 177–180, 189 *et seq.*, 297, 300
    compensation order and, 177–180, 189–191, 297, 300
    conditions for, 174
    contents, 178, 297
    encumbrances, effect on, 178, 180, 297
    EEC right of establishment and, 212, 213
    extinguishment of rights, etc., compensation, 178–180, 189 *et seq.*, 297, 300
    liabilities, effect on, 178, 179, 297
    minority protection, 184, 186, 187, 295
    national interest, necessary in, 173, 294
    nationalisation measures, similarity, 180, 181
    notices extending to other holdings, 186, 187, 295
    Parliamentary control, 184, 188, 296
    prohibition order, following, 174, 294
    relevant body corporate—
      meaning, 175, 294
      share or loan capital, 174, 177, 294
    rights, effect on, 178, 297
    safeguarding provisions, 182–185, 297
    transfer of rights etc. under, 178, 179, 297

MINISTER. *See* GOVERNMENT; SECRETARY OF STATE

NATIONAL ENTERPRISE BOARD,
accounting year, meaning, 318
accounts and audit, 335
agent—
  Crown, of, not regarded as, 24, 283
  Government department, of, may be, 25, 286
Annual Report, 336
  directions included under—
    s. 3 . . . 89, 90, 285
    s. 7 . . . 63, 288A
  register of members' interests to be annexed, 23, 336
annual review, 71
body corporate, 325
borrowing powers, 71, 329
  wholly owned subsidiaries, by, 69, 331
Capital Debt, 334
  acquisition under s. 3 direction, expenses of, 96, 334
chairman and deputy, 16, 283, 321
circulars relating to investments, distribution, 328
composition, 17, 18, 283
contractual liability, effect of subsequent direction, 93, 285

NATIONAL ENTERPRISE BOARD
—cont.
Corporate Plan, 71
Crown privilege inapplicable, 24, 283
directions by Secretary of State to, 29, 62, 63, 288A
  general, 62, 63, 288A
  specific, 30, 62, 63, 288A
duty, etc., or other charge, not exempt, 26, 283
establishment, 1, 16, 283
execution of instruments and contracts, 325
financial assistance under Industry Act, 1972, by, 55, 69, 73 *et seq.*, 285, 342–344
  delegation by Secretary of State, 74, 87, 89–93, 285
financial duties, 57
  determination by Secretary of State as to, 57–61, 288
financial limits on powers, 68–70, 289
  general external borrowing, as to, 69, 289
  interest outstanding not included, 69, 289
  loan guarantees, 69, 289
  public dividend capital, 69, 289, 333
  statutory limit, 68, 69, 289
  Treasury guarantees not repaid, 69, 289
functions, 28, 35
  establishment, etc., of industrial undertakings, 35, 36–39, 284
  extension of public ownership, 22, 35, 41–44, 153, 284
  promotion of—
    industrial democracy, 35, 50, 284
    reorganisation of industry, 35, 40, 284
Government—
  control, 71
  financial liability to, 95–97, 285
  investment in, 69, 333
  loans to, 71, 329, 330
guarantees on loans to, 69, 289, 332
industrial democracy, power to promote, 35, 50, 284
industrial undertaking—
  establishment, maintenance, etc., of, 35, 36–39, 284
  meaning, 36, 318
jurisdiction, 30, 52, 284
loans to, 71, 329, 330
members, 16–18, 283
  appointment, 16, 283, 321
  interests—
    Board contracts, in, 20, 324
    disclosure, 19–23, 321, 324
    public, 22, 23, 283
    financial, 19, 321
    register of financial, 23, 283
  Members of Parliament, disqualified from being, 323
  remuneration, 322
  tenure, 321

References are to paragraph numbers

127

References are to paragraph numbers

References are to paragraph numbers

PRINTED IN GREAT BRITAIN BY OFFSET LITHOGRAPHY BY
BILLING & SONS LTD, GUILDFORD, LONDON AND WORCESTER